the art of Marguerite Stix

Richard McLanathan

the art of Marguerite Stix

HARRY N. ABRAMS, INC., *PUBLISHERS,* NEW YORK

Edited by Theresa C. Brakeley

Designed by Ladislav Svatos / Graphicon Ltd.

Library of Congress Cataloging in Publication Data

McLanathan, Richard B.
    The art of Marguerite Stix.

    Bibliography: p.
    Includes index.
    1. Stix, Marguerite. I. Title.
N6811.5.S76M32   709'.2'4   77-9089
ISBN 0-8109-1620-7

Library of Congress Catalogue Card Number: 77-9089

Published in 1977 by Harry N. Abrams, Incorporated, New York
All rights reserved. No part of the contents of this book may be
reproduced without the written permission of the publishers

Printed and bound in Japan

Frontispiece: *Self-portrait.* 1957. Pastel, 24 x 19″. Collection the author

CONTENTS

foreword

13 Vandam Street, New York

The artist's presence was as palpable as the clear light flooding the L-shaped studio through tall windows, offering glimpses of a walled garden rich with ivy, and the slanting skylight overhead, illuminating the work table covered with shell fragments partly shaped on an emery wheel which seemed to have been in use but moments before, the working drawings close at hand.

Tossed over the back of a red chair, a violet, magenta, and green silk scarf. Nearby a red-and-green-striped apron and an easel with just-used palette and brushes, pastels and drawing materials, watercolors. Jars and canisters of small shells, separated by color, and of pearls, sorted by size and shape; small containers of gems, precious and semiprecious—the palette of yet another medium. Philodendrons in clay pots climbing upward toward the light.

On shelves, sculptures in bronze: Lincoln's brooding head, Lincoln mounted on a small horse, figures of dancers, of women and children, in groups and singly; and, in plaster: the head of a friend, a self-portrait, a head of the artist's husband, a life-size portrait bust of a woman, elegant and sad; female figures, seated and standing. In a glass case: painted terra cottas—a Nativity, a Descent from the Cross, a swimming hole, bathers, a jazz combo, groups and single figures; wood carvings, figural also, some heightened with the same fresh color as the terra cottas; compositions in pierced brass.

Cases full of books on art, philosophy, music, literature in several languages, including The Odyssey, Aesop's Fables, Alice in Wonderland, Sandburg's Lincoln, Sartre, Gide, Camus, volumes old and new. Metal cabinets full of drawings, watercolors, pastels, sketches in ink, Conté crayon, pencil, with pen or brush, in a line at once free yet controlled, personal as a signature, especially in the drawings of shells and of the beloved ruins of the old Dutch plantation house on the island of St. John, Virgin Islands, where the Stixes made their vacation home for many years.

The walls papered with pastels, oils, watercolors; brilliant flower pieces in a gamut of moods; landscapes of Martha's Vineyard, Greenwich Village, the Atlantic coast of South America, the island of St. John; drawings of Europa and a languishing bull, Orpheus and Eurydice, the Judgment of Paris, Apollo driving the chariot of the sun, Apollo pursuing Daphne, the Fall of Icarus, the Rhine Maidens, Cleopatra and the asp, Marilyn Monroe as the Penitent Magdalen, in scenes of black and white, in full color, or touched with color; and the self-portraits, both in color and in black and white, which seem to appraise the observer even as they are being observed.

3 Marguerite creating a sculptural abstraction with shells, 1964

4 Working materials for shell jewelry

Europe

1907–1941

Marguerite Stix was born Margret Christine Salzer in Vienna on June 15, 1907. Her family was well established, solid, bourgeois, with the mixture of central European backgrounds typical of the city. As in almost all Jewish families living in the imperial capital, she was brought up in an atmosphere of awareness of music, theater, literature, dance, painting, sculpture. In her youth she studied both ballet and voice.

Vienna was a crossroads of East and West, a magnet which drew all sorts of variously gifted persons, especially from central, southern, and eastern Europe. There, in the autumnal years of the Austro-Hungarian monarchy and in the troubled times of the republic that followed its collapse, an extraordinary flowering of the arts occurred. Writers and composers, architects and painters and sculptors knew one another and often met and collaborated. Café life was extremely lively and much involved with the arts. Leading salons were made up of a brilliant combination of literary, musical, artistic, and scientific abilities—multilingual, diverse, urbane, knowing what was going on in the rest of Europe and even far away in the United States.

Vienna's cultural vitality encompassed many conflicting movements and developments. The city worshiped its traditional talents, yet somehow provided an atmosphere in which experiment was possible, not only in the arts but also in medicine. The theories of Freud had given new direction to creative search. Artur Schnitzler's cool dissections of society in fiction and in the theater contrasted with the still strong cult of conservative Romanticism that championed the music of Mahler, which, in turn, was completely opposed to the twelve-tone innovations of Schönberg and Webern. The Surrealist fiction of Kafka somehow coexisted with Franz Lehar's *Merry Widow,* the Imperial Academy with the rebellious Sezession. There was room for the birth of Zionism in a milieu which harbored both anti-Semitism and large numbers of gifted Jews; for the fantastic ballets and cinema scripts of Hugo von Hofmannsthal and the operas conceived by him with Richard Strauss; for the satirist, poet, playwright, and critic Karl Kraus and the group that met at the Café Griensteidl; for the pioneering architecture of Otto Wagner and of Adolf Loos, who tried (with only occasional success, despite a large popular following) to change the life style of an era; and especially for Josef Hoffmann, Wagner's leading successor in architecture and the most protean and magisterial cultural figure of the period.

Marguerite remembered Hoffmann as "a genius and *bon vivant*...whose name is linked with an Austrian venture to organize the talent of young artists. Under his encouragement they created beautiful objects and influenced older artists to use their proven craftsmanship to

7

8

enhance their modern projects. The name of this colorful group...all inspired by the enthusiasm, the indomitable spirit, the resourcefulness, the imagination, the salesmanship (on an elegant level but inescapable, nevertheless) of Josef Hoffmann...was Wiener Werkstätte."[1] As Marguerite recalled, "At the time I knew Hoffmann, I was first too young to be a member of the group, but I diligently studied art, and he was our leader—not only because of his great talent but also because of his superiority as a person of instinctive realization of the needs and aspirations of other artists. A great promoter of art with an enormous *joie de vivre!*"

Hoffmann, with the architect and designer Kolomon Moser, who was also a founder of the Sezession, and the young merchant Fritz Wärndorfer, established the Wiener Werkstätte in 1903. It was created following the precedent already set in England by the example of William Morris, of Charles Albert Ashbee's Guild of Handicrafts, of the work in architecture and design of Charles Rennie Mackintosh in Glasgow and of Henri van de Velde and the Maison Moderne in Paris. Sculptors, painters, architects, cabinetmakers, typographers, bookbinders, leatherworkers, glassworkers, graphic artists, metalworkers, enamelists, mosaicists, makers of stained-glass windows, and designers of furniture, textiles, and wallpaper—all were a part of the active team of expert craftsmen and -women who made up the Werkstätte. Also in close relation were the ceramists of the Wiener Keramik studio, established three years later by Michael Powolny, Austria's leading artist in this field, and Berthold Löffler, a pupil of Moser who was also a well-known graphic designer.

The state schools of glass and of ceramics were invigorated by the example and activity of the Werkstätte, which, in turn, became a model for the Bauhaus and a number of other similar institutions. Its program and philosophy were more widely influential still, not only in Europe but also in America. The Werkstätte was a major element in the vitally creative world in which Marguerite spent her formative years, and for the rest of her life she drew on that experience and stimulation.

Marguerite learned to read French and German by the age of four. She read voraciously, everything she could lay her hands on in the house of a cultured family with intellectual interests, "with books under the pillows of my bed," she later recalled, "so I could catch any chance as soon or late as I could see."[1] At the outbreak of World War I, when she was sent off to stay with her maternal grandparents in Innsbruck, her constant companions were books and an enormous Saint Bernard dog named Tasso, after the great Italian poet of the sixteenth century. Because of the disruptions of war and the economic and social upheavals

9

7 Martha and Siegfried Salzer, Marguerite's mother and father

8 Marguerite as a baby in Vienna

9 Marguerite with Tasso in Innsbruck

10

11

accompanying it, she had a lonely childhood, and her passion for literature and the arts led to a precocious maturity. "I had from early in my life," she wrote in 1972, "the drive to create drawings and sculpture, and that was the only way to stop my restlessness, so I had no choice."[1]

    While still in her teens, she applied for admission to the Kunstgewerbeschule, the official art school of Vienna, but was turned down because of her youth. The faculty of the school, however, impressed with the ability shown by the work she submitted, became interested in her, and, young as she was, she was accepted as a member of the group which surrounded Josef Hoffmann, who remained a devoted friend and admirer throughout his life. From then on, to the considerable dismay of her parents, she spent almost all her time with this otherwise all-male group in coffeehouses and wine gardens, sketching, talking,

10 Michael Powolny and his ceramics class, Marguerite at far right

11 *Josef Hoffmann.* Sketch by Emil Orlik

12 Female figure formed over pots thrown by Lucie Gomperz (Dame Lucie Rie). 1925. Ceramic, over life size. Shown at Austrian pavilion, Exposition Internationale des Arts décoratifs et industriels, 1925; destroyed by bombing of Vienna, 1945

13

13 Mirror frame. c. 1930. Ceramic.
Destroyed by bombing of Vienna, 1945

14 Bowl. c. 1925. Glazed ceramic.
Destroyed by bombing of Vienna, 1945

12   14

listening, observing—knowing instinctively that the experience was not only fascinating but also invaluable for her future.

When she finally entered art school as a regular student, she did extremely well and graduated with the highest honors. Afterward she continued with sculpture and ceramics. Her work was shown in major exhibitions, and she received a number of important commissions, including one for a larger-than-life-size ceramic figure, in scale alone a *tour de force*. This figure won a prize at the World Exposition of 1925 in Paris, where it was featured in the Austrian Pavilion, designed by Hoffmann in collaboration with Oskar Strnad.

Following the Werkstätte example, she made many functional objects, such as a large ceramic stove with glazed decorations and mirror frames in the form of wreaths of graceful figures, enigmatic in mood, carried out with quiet virtuosity. Her pots and vases tended generally to simple shapes with somewhat rough glazes and expressionistic decorations. She also did ceramic portraits and *putto* heads reflecting the influence of Powolny's colorful pottery, such as his *Four Seasons* of 1908 (Österreichisches Museum für Angewandte Kunst). In addition, she modeled quaintly costumed figures suggesting the picturesque carvings, often in painted limewood, of Franz Barwig, who, between 1925 and 1927, sculptured many details for the buildings of the Merriwether Post estate, "Mar-a-Lago," in Palm Beach, Florida, the concept of Josef Urban, a Viennese designer who later produced sets for the Ziegfeld Follies and the Metropolitan Opera in New York.

Marguerite was also immensely busy with sculptures in bronze, iron, and other metals. She exhibited regularly, both locally and in Venice, Brussels, Munich, Paris, and other major cities. Early she achieved a reputation for portrait sculpture, especially of children. For three years she collaborated with Michael Powolny on various state projects, including

15 Buttons. 1938–40. Ceramic

16 Buttons and pins made for the Paris *haute couture*. 1939–40. Ceramic. Metropolitan Museum of Art, New York City

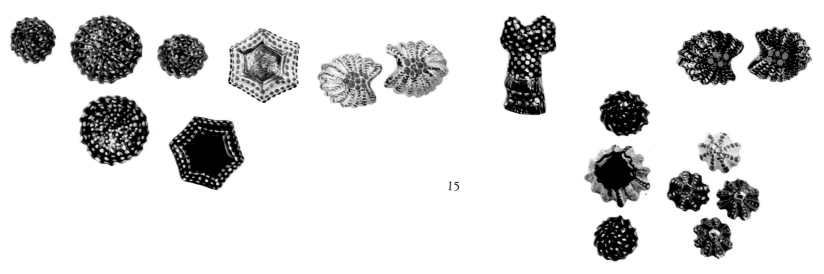

15

architectural monuments and garden decorations, for she was always interested in architecture and landscape design. On other projects she collaborated with such diverse artists as Anton Faistauer (a friend of Gustav Klimt and Egon Schiele), whose painted decorations in the Festspielhaus in Salzburg were destroyed by the Nazis in 1938 as degenerate; with the Czech sculptor Anton Hanak, who contributed to many of Hoffmann's architectural projects and is perhaps best known for his immense monument to Kemal Atatürk in Ankara; with Adolf Loos; with Clemens Holzmeister, a major pupil of Loos whose designs were also realized at Ankara; and with such other architects and designers as the versatile Josef Wimmer (a member of the Werkstätte, who later taught at the Chicago Art Institute), Oskar Strnad, and, of course, Hoffmann himself.

In the meantime, like Hoffmann and many others, Marguerite designed for the outstanding glass firm of J. and L. Lobmayer and the Augarten porcelain manufactory, both still in existence, and for Goldscheider Keramik. She added to her experience during extended visits to Paris with study at the Académie de la Grande Chaumière and in the studios of Charles Despiau and Antoine Bourdelle. In 1928 she successfully showed a group of her Paris watercolors at the Wiener Werkbundt and at other galleries. During these years a number of her works in various media were acquired for the permanent collection of the Kunstgewerbemuseum, Vienna's Museum of Arts and Industries, which was demolished by Russian bombing in World War II.

As a protégée of Hoffmann and Powolny, she met the leading poets, playwrights, critics, painters, sculptors, and musicians and knew the work of many whom she had not met personally, not only Austrians but also visitors to Vienna such as the maverick pioneer American architect Frank Lloyd Wright and Mackintosh. She grew up knowing the paintings of Klimt and Schiele, of Richard Gerstl and Oskar Kokoschka. She frequented exhibitions at the Sezession, the institution founded in 1897 in reaction to the opulence, the parade, and the essential conservatism of the Kunstlerhaus, which had become over the years an increasingly insensitive and retardant organization. At the Sezession she saw the exhibitions of the livelier local artists and the avant-garde of Europe in galleries with movable partitions and flexible lighting. The building, now regarded as a landmark of modern architecture, was designed in 1897 by the gifted Wagner pupil Josef Maria Olbrich, at the age of thirty, with, in his own words, "walls white and shining, holy and modest."

Almost all Vienna's artists were used to turning their hands to a great variety of endeavors. Architects followed the precedent of Otto Wagner, who designed not only important buildings but also lighting fixtures, furniture, and other elements of their interiors. Artists in all fields worked in cooperative effort toward the realization of large projects, a classic example being Hoffmann's Palais Stoclet in Brussels. It included the work of Klimt and a dozen other artists and craftsmen in diverse media, carrying out the precepts of the Werkstätte, according to which every part that served to create the whole was considered worthy of the professional attention of the most gifted of designers. The result, as in the Renaissance, when a similar attitude prevailed, was a consistency of quality and imagination, whether the final work were a catalogue of an exhibition at the Sezession, a theatrical poster, tableware, textiles, jewelry, ecclesiastical objects, or whatever. For the Palais Stoclet Hoffmann designed not only the building but also chairs, tables, cases, floor treatments, wallpapers, draperies, ceramics, and glass. The universality of the approach, the idea of the central responsibility of the designer for the *ambiente* of life—these were a significant heritage of the Werkstätte.

During these years Marguerite married Dr. Bela von Gomperz, who had been a close friend of the writer Peter Altenberg and was a member of the intellectual and musical circles of Vienna. The marriage lasted only a few years, for her high professional competence and independence as an artist seem to have been a challenge to the more traditionally minded doctor, but it enlarged her acquaintance, and she continued successfully with her career until the sudden and devastating revolution when the Nazis took over Vienna in March of 1938.

With almost no warning she and her family had to flee. Losing track of one another in the confusion of the Nazi *putsch,* she managed to catch the last train for Paris before the borders were closed, while her father, mother, and grandmother, as she learned only after some years, took a train for the Far East, where they had friends and relatives, but they were forced off the train in Poland and died there in a concentration camp. As for the work of her early years, all was destroyed by the Russian bombing of Vienna at the end of World War II.

She arrived in Paris penniless. Money she had entrusted to a friend bound for England never arrived. Fortunately, she found members of the Rie family, distant cousins, who knew her capability in ceramics. With their help she found a place to stay and access to a kiln, so that she could carry on her career, and she began designing a line of ceramic pins and buttons in the fanciful, figural style she had practiced in Vienna. Because of the war no metal was available, and her unique ceramic creations were an immediate success with the *haute couture* of Paris, resulting in commissions from almost every leading house, among them Molyneux, Balenciaga, Schiaparelli, Lanvin, and Patou.

17

Her respite was to be short-lived. In June of 1940 German armor was rolling toward Paris, virtually unimpeded by the defeated forces of a demoralized France. Feigning pregnancy to get through the lines, she fled south to join the Ries near Clermont-Ferrand, but she was seized by the French authorities as an enemy alien and interned in the infamous concentration camp at Gurs, near the Spanish border, where so many escaping Spanish Loyalists were imprisoned.

There she recorded her experiences in a group of drawings done in the only medium available to her—lipstick and ink. Without malice or sentimentality the drawings show the life of the twenty-five thousand women interned because they were foreign-born, though all had been pro-French, and most had had sons, fathers, or husbands fighting for France. The attempts of these women to maintain some semblance of dignity in a dehumanizing

17-19 Drawings made in the concentration camp at Gurs. 1940. Lipstick and ink, diameter 7″ (17 and 19) and 5¾″ (18). Collection Hugh Stix, New York City

environment, where, in Marguerite's words, "civilization and nature had closed their doors," find a moving expression in these drawings of human response under inhuman conditions.

On July 19 she was released, but without her identification papers, lost by the authorities (conveniently, no doubt, because they established that she was neither German nor an enemy). As she wrote later of the day of her release: "At last the gates opened to make me free. I had been warned that I would not be able to get transportation..., that even the camp, with all its terrors, would be better than to be errant on the road. ... I stayed on the road to try to stop a car. ... I stood outside the camp from 11 A.M. until 7 P.M. in the pouring rain and waited. ... I think then I was at the lowest point of my adventures. ... But ... a very elegant car, which approached so quickly that I had not noticed its coming, stopped before me. I could hardly believe it ..., the dream of ugliness was over. ... The car sped through a peaceful and gracious country. ... Everything ... seemed too beautiful to be true ...; it seemed to me that I had lived for a long time in complete darkness."[2]

During the following months Marguerite lived here and there in southern France. For some weeks she cooked for a group of Czech Protestant ministers, also refugees, living on a remote farm in the mountains. They arranged for her to receive a Czech passport, under the name of Margarita Gomperzova, and other papers, so that in the autumn of 1940 she finally, despite the vigilance of Franco's Spain, reached Lisbon, which was already full to overflowing with refugees desperate to escape a troubled Europe.

Carefully made plans to go to the Belgian Congo failed at the last moment; then, after weeks of waiting, she received an American visa. Seeking passage to the United States, she haunted the bars and taverns along the waterfront most frequented by officers and sailors of the merchant marine. Early in March, 1941, she met the captain of a cork transport, whose usual run was between Portugal and England but who was about to make his first voyage across the Atlantic. His ship, the S.S. Melo, was small, with a crew of thirty-seven. Marguerite, officially traveling second class, was the only passenger. The voyage was not uneventful, since the vessel was stopped and searched several times at sea. After four rough weeks they landed at Baltimore. It was the first time either she or the captain had ever been in America, and they celebrated their safe arrival with dinner ashore at a waterfront restaurant.

Then she boarded a bus for New York. Well after midnight she arrived in Times Square, again almost penniless. Though she knew a few people in the city, she was on her own.

■

paintings and drawings

1941–1974

In New York Marguerite found freelance art work and then, because of her knowledge of ceramics, got a job as foreman and kiln master at a Hummel porcelain-figure factory on the Bowery, where she worked from six in the morning until eight at night, stacking and unloading the huge kiln. In 1943 she went to work for the Charlton Lamp Company, on Greene Street, for whom she painted porcelain lamp bases during a less exhausting day. In the evenings and on weekends she painted tiles and porcelain boxes, which she showed in her tiny studio-workshop at 134 MacDougal Street, next door to the house she lived in, known as a landmark because it was once the home of Louisa May Alcott. She also continued to create the ceramic fashion accessories with which she had earned her way before her flight from Paris. Her work attracted attention, and gradually she began to sell through Bergdorf Goodman and other shops, and with this encouragement she began to think of resuming an artistic career.

It was at this time that she met Hugh Stix, whom she later married. In 1946 she gave up her job and devoted full time to her own work, turning particularly to drawing and painting. A new and totally different chapter in her life had begun.

For some years during the 1950s the Stixes spent many Sundays with Hugh's parents at their country house in Westchester. Each time, whenever there was anything blooming in the garden, they went back to New York with armfuls of flowers. Marguerite could not resist their appeal and often spent the next few days, from first light until dark, painting them as she had arranged them on her return—in a stoneware pitcher, a green glass vase, a pewter tankard, or some salt-glazed crock or jar she had found in country antique stores in Pennsylvania. She never placed the flowers in a carefully considered light but put them wherever they looked well around the house and studio and then drew and painted them as they were. Often Hugh would come home late in the day to find her still at work, trying to make yet one more study before the light had entirely failed.

The range of mood in her flower paintings is broad, as it is in the rest of her work, though they tend far more to bright color, with a brilliant immediacy of handling. They show considerable variation in tone: a few are somber, others pensive, still others, the majority, exuberantly gay. Some are vigorously structured in black, while others are carried out entirely in color; some are relieved against the white of the paper, while others have backgrounds of modulated watercolor washes or vibrant strokes of crayon or pastel. In all their variety they are essentially celebrations of nature, which seemed, as she so poignantly felt after her liberation from the concentration camp years before, "too beautiful to be true."

The remembrance of the "complete darkness" of that experience never left her, nor the shadow of the fate of her family, friends, and all the others who did not escape. Her awareness and her sensibility to nature were heightened by those memories.

Her paintings were never brought to such a state of realization as to limit the dimension of implication she sought. They were complete when she considered the statement made. She worked swiftly and surely, almost without hesitation, changing from oil to crayon, to pastel, to watercolor and back, and occasionally mixing media or turning to drawing with complete freedom. Then, during the next day or so, she carefully considered them and, with admirable objectivity, destroyed the greater number as not being up to the standard she had set. In looking at the remaining works, one cannot but respect the rigor of that standard and yet feel regret for the loss of at least some of those that were culled.

In a separate category from the rest of her work is a group of drawings and paintings, some in glazed ceramic, of cityscapes, interiors, and still lifes, many at small scale. There are pastel views of the living room on MacDougal Street, glowing with warm color; and, in drawings touched with color, the familiar furniture and household objects are transformed into tightly integrated compositions unified by linear pattern or by tone. A number of glazed tile paintings with views of Greenwich Village, done during the 1940s, are miniature in size, yet completely realized.

20 *MacDougal Street.* 1948. Painted tile, 4 x 4″. Collection Mr. and Mrs. Andrew Scarsi, New York

21 *Interior, Macdougal Street.* 1949. Painted tile, 4 x 4″. Collection Hugh Stix, New York City

Flowers. 1952. Pastel, 24 x 18".
Collection Mr. and Mrs. Leonard C.
Hirsch, New York City

Stix

Flowers. 1954. Pastel, 24 x 18″.
Washington Irving Gallery,
New York City

Later she painted tiles at larger scale, also with city scenes and with still-life subjects as well, many in a broader manner. In this style she decorated a set of china with designs incorporating objects from her own kitchen and dining room, including the vegetables, fruits, and other ingredients of the expertly cooked meals for which she was well known. The china service was an inexpensive set, like those used in hotels and restaurants, which she had bought to show an artist friend the technique of ceramic painting and glazing. When an unexpected commission took him away from New York for an extended period, she decorated the entire lot in color, had all the plates, cups, and dishes refired, and often used them when entertaining friends. The designs are freely brushed with a sure hand. Though no two are alike, the set is unified by color, scale, and style and forms an enchanting whole.

In a related manner Marguerite painted tile tabletops, including one showing a part of her kitchen, with lamp, coffeepot, chair, and the table strewn with the items for a meal in preparation. Another, later one has a design of leeks, apples, an artichoke, and a pear scattered on a tablecloth of embroidery and lace, with faint echoes in both color and pattern of the sinuous decorative style of Klimt.

26 Fifty-piece set of china, painted and refired. 1949. Minnesota Museum of Art, St. Paul

27 *Interior, MacDougal Street.* 1950. Painted tiles, 16 x 12". Minnesota Museum of Art, St. Paul

Her technical command, whatever the medium she chose, was always such that even her smallest sketches have a satisfying completeness. The landscapes, whether of Martha's Vineyard, the coast of South America, or the Virgin Islands, often rendered in soft watercolor washes, have a distinctive character resulting from her perception of the particular qualities of each place and her feeling for it. There is never anything pretentious about the paintings; they are there, directly apprehended, felt, and recorded in her own personal terms—lyric, appreciative, reflective of deep enjoyment.

The drawings are often yet more spontaneous. In them her line becomes even more individual, especially in the black-and-white sketches of St. John, with the ruins of the eighteenth-century plantation house, the garden with its luxuriance of growth, its hibiscus and bougainvillea, and the two pavilions, joined by a paved patio, which form the modern dwelling. In these the black line wanders briefly and lovingly, delineating and suggesting the familiar scene, with always a slightly differing nuance of light or season. Almost always the central feature is the turpentine tree. Around it revolve most of the compositions, whether painted or drawn, of St. John. Full of character, with its attendant orchids, air-nurtured, the tree does, indeed, dominate the site, casting its shadow across the ruins, the basic structure of the garden that Marguerite planned and planted, with terraces on the foundations of mansion and outbuildings alike, and the low remnants of the ancient walls clad in vines and shaded by other trees. The old Dutch graveyard nearby, with its massive, simple stones marking the burials of long forgotten members of the De Nully family, many of them children, also figures again and again in the drawings and paintings of St. John, the island home where so many friends were entertained, so many designs and sketches were made, and so many projects planned.

Mythical and legendary subjects, almost entirely in black and white, are numerous in Marguerite's imagery. They are concerned chiefly with motives from classical mythology, though there are occasional Biblical themes and legends of the North. One series treats of episodes from the story of Cleopatra; another cryptically illustrates fables from Aesop, La Fontaine, and European folklore. The mood varies from a *Europa* with a fatuously simpering, amorous bull to a somber and haunted *Oedipus* group. The medium is usually pencil, black Conté crayon, or pen and ink. In a very few instances there are passages of color in pastel or wash. The quality of line ranges from the swift, flowing strokes of some of the *Rhine Maiden, Orpheus,* and *Apollo* groups (which are closely related in style to her sculptures in pierced brass plaques) to the firm, dark, more structural touches that delineate figures and establish major

28 *Still Life.* 1952. Crayon and pencil, 17 x 14". Grand Rapids Art Museum, Grand Rapids, Michigan

Stix

Scene looking north from roof at
MacDougal Street. 1950. Watercolor,
11½ x 15″. Collection Mr. and Mrs.

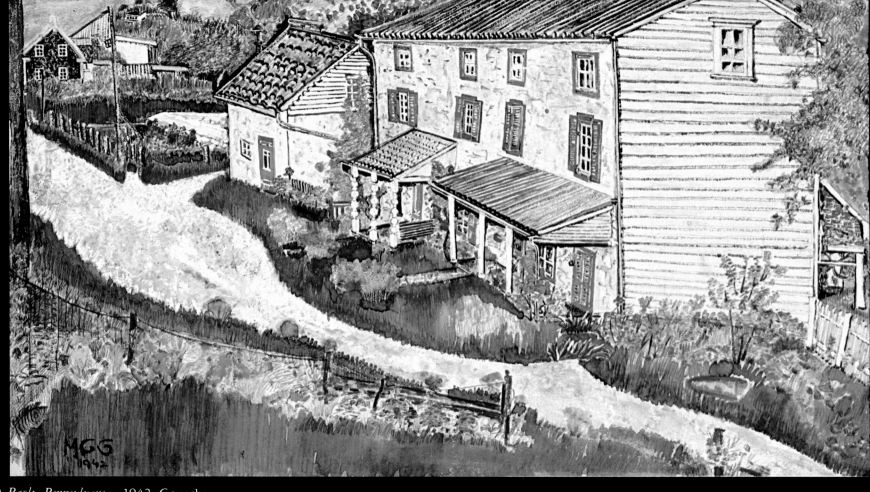

0 *Paoli, Pennsylvania.* 1942. Gouache.
11½ x 20". Collection Mr. and Mrs
Howard A. Seitz, New York City

Stix

31 *Self-portrait.* 1961. Pastel, 24 x 20".
Collection Hugh Stix, New York City

Self-portrait. 1961. Pastel, 24 x 20″.
Collection Hugh Stix, New York City

33 *Self-portrait*. 1958. Ink, 24 x 18".
Washington Irving Gallery,
New York City

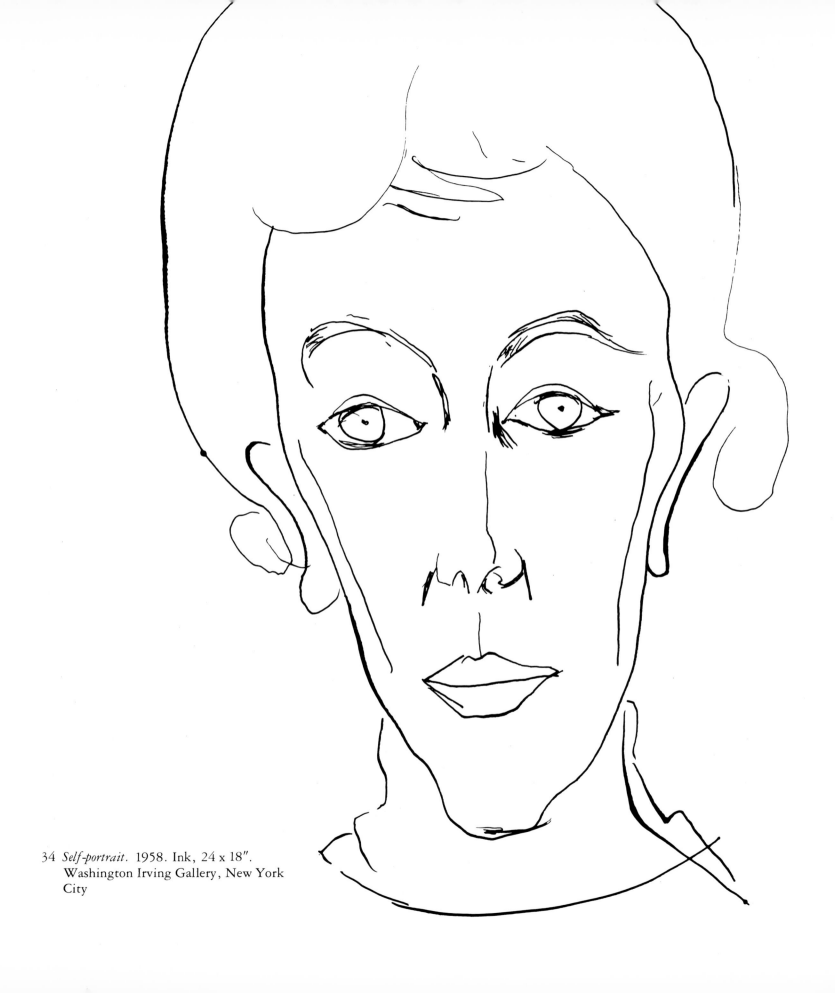

34 *Self-portrait.* 1958. Ink, 24 x 18″.
Washington Irving Gallery, New York
City

35 *Self-portrait*. 1962. Pastel, 24 x 18"
Minnesota Museum of Art, St. Paul

6 *Self-portrait.* 1961. Pastel, 24 x 20″.
Collection Hugh Stix, New York City

37

37 *Self-portrait*. 1960. Conté crayon, 24 x
      19″. The Columbia Museum of Art,
      Columbia, South Carolina

38 *Self-portrait*. 1959. Ink, 22 x 14″.
      Tennessee Botanical Gardens and Fine
      Arts Center, Nashville

39 *Self-portrait*. 1958. Ink, 24 x 18″.
      Washington Irving Gallery,
      New York City

Stux

38   39

43

Stix

40 *Self-portrait*. 1962. Pastel and cray
18 x 14½". Washington Irving
Gallery, New York City

Self-portrait. 1962. Pastel and crayon,
19 x 14½". Washington Irving
Gallery, New York City

aspects of the design, as in many of the *Theseus* drawings and some of the *Orpheus* versions. Beyond being descriptive, the line is often highly decorative, enriching the flat pattern of the drawings—an effect that was obviously important to Marguerite—and enhanced by the deliberately unnaturalistic and variable spatial system she employed.

The style of these drawings is even more idiosyncratic than in those she did on the island of St. John. Firm and finite forms, often considerably abstract, mingle and contrast with those which deliquesce, seemingly caught in a curious state of transformation as if some Circe-like magic were at work. Small floating shapes, organic but scarcely identifiable, intermix with the figures, and occasionally large-eyed apparitions lend a further Surrealist dimension to the generally dreamlike world of velleities, emotions, and sometimes Freudian ambiguities and recondite symbolism that the drawings conjure up.

42 *Washington Square, New York.* 1948. Ink, 7¼ x 7½". Washington Irving Gallery, New York City

43 *Sixth Avenue Shop, New York.* 1948. Ink, 4¼ x 5¼". Washington Irving Gallery, New York City

42

43

44 *Bleecker Street, New York.* 1948. Ink,
   7¾ x 8¾″. Washington Irving Gallery,
   New York City

45 *Washington Square, New York.* 1948.
   Ink, 7½ x 8″. Washington Irving
   Gallery, New York City

46 *Washington Square, New York.* 1948.
   Ink, 3¾ x 4½″. Washington Irving
   Gallery, New York City

47 *Harbor Scene, New York.* 1948. Ink,
   5 x 7½″. Washington Irving Gallery,
   New York City

45

44

46

47

Stix

48 *Trunk Bay, St. John.* 1965. Ink, 10½ x
    12½". Collection Virginia Field,
    New York City

49 *The House at DeNully Hill, St. John.*
    1965. Ink, 11 x 23". Collection Hugh
    Stix, New York City

Marguerite's drawings and paintings must be considered together, because she returned often to similar and related subjects, creating variations on a theme, each in a different mood and often varying also in medium—sometimes in black and white, sometimes touched with color, sometimes essentially painterly, being conceived and realized entirely in color. This is notable in the sequence of her self-portraits, done over a period of several years.

The series devoted to Marilyn Monroe also involves the whole spectrum. Touched by the unfulfilled hopes of the actress's life and the pathos of her death, Marguerite cast her in these studies as the Penitent Mary Magdalene, seated before a mirror and contemplating a skull. The motive is a traditional one in the history of art, being perhaps most familiarly employed by the French seventeenth-century artist Georges de la Tour. And there are echoes of La Tour's several versions of the subject in Marguerite's drawings and paintings. Though the compositions are all very similar, there are minor variations in the position of the head, the hands, and the partially draped figure. The subject, facing the viewer's left, sits at her theatrical dressing table, its looking glass surrounded by glowing light bulbs, the skull before her. She never looks into the glass but almost always gazes sadly, often despairingly, out at us. The mirror does not reflect the naturalistically correct image of the young woman in front of it but shows her in profile, looking down, sometimes merely pensive, at others, spectral. In most of the versions the skull is grinning demonically, suggesting the inexorability for her of death, but is never itself reflected, as if the alter ego beyond the glass were also beyond the domain of death.

Some renditions of the subject are in black and white, mostly in ink, but the greater number employ color, often brilliant, in pastel, oil, or watercolor, with occasionally a mixture of these media. There is great variety in the color schemes: glowing ochers and oranges; deep blues, grays, and muted purple; highly keyed pinks, blues, and yellows. In all of them the feeling is conveyed as much by the color as by form. And, as in all Marguerite's work, the frequent darkly shadowed passages in black have a baleful implication. Throughout the series the actress is presented not as a portrait but—as revealed by her facial expression, her lassitude, and the gentleness of her hands, which sometimes hold the grotesque skull almost tenderly—in her helplessness as a victim.

Animals of all kinds, fantastic and real, recur throughout Marguerite's work, especially in the drawings of mythical and legendary subjects. From earliest childhood she had been fascinated by animals, and after her marriage to Hugh Stix she and he went frequently to the Bronx Zoo, where she made innumerable sketches from life, followed by many more studies

50 *Turpentine Tree, DeNully Hill,* 1965. Ink, 15 x 12". Collection Hugh Stix, New York City

51

52

51 *Marilyn Monroe.* 1962. Pastel, 24 x 18″.
   Art Collection, University of Maine,
   Orono

52 *Marilyn Monroe.* 1962. Pastel, 24 x 18″.
   Washington Irving Gallery,
   New York City

53 *Marilyn Monroe.* 1962. Pastel, 24 x 18″.
   Tennessee Botanical Gardens and Fine
   Arts Center, Nashville

from memory. Horses seem to have had a particular interest for her. She sculptured them, drew and painted them, sometimes as expressions of natural power, as in the plunging, rearing chargers pulling the chariot of the sun at headlong pace, or, in another mood, as delicately modeled, elegantly sculptured thoroughbreds, or, in still another aspect, as the tremulous insecurity of the young zebra and the newborn donkey, long remembered and realized at last in bronze.

The subject of *Orpheus Taming the Beasts* with the music of his lyre may have attracted her just because of the animals that are an integral part of the composition, on which she wrought many variations. Or it may have had some special symbolism or personal meaning involving the sources of her creative imagination and her instinctive affinities with the natural world. Sometimes Orpheus appears as a kind of warlock, weaving powerful spells to charm the crowding animals, whose savagery gleams in their ferocious eyes. Sometimes he is a courtly magician, enchanting them with softer and subtler musical incantations while lost in a private world of unearthly harmony. But always the eyes of the beasts seem to burn in the surrounding shadows, suggesting the extent and the force of the powers spellbound by the demigod's uncanny skill, taught him by the Muses.

Everything about this category of drawings is totally unreal, abundantly imaginative, full of invention and vivid expression. The compositions are endlessly varied, rhythmic, rich with formal resonances and with reticular or curving, spiraling passages, all achieved with a flowing, flexible line, capable of nuance, modulation, and structural subtlety. The mode is consistently fantastic and expressive of feeling, which is conveyed as much by the nonobjective aspects of the design as by the representational, for the mythological, legendary, or historical title often serves simply as a gloss or a point of departure. The content is layered and multifold, the underlying subjects being personal and often enigmatic, alive with implications and overtones. Essentially poetic, these drawings, like so much of Marguerite's creative work, are constantly reminiscent of music.

■

54 *Marilyn Monroe.* 1962. Ink with felt pen, 24 x 18". Washington Irving Gallery, New York City

55 *The Judgment of Paris.* 1961. Ink, 22
14". The Columbia Museum of Art,
Columbia, South Carolina

The Judgment of Paris. 1961. Pencil and crayon, 24 x 19". Collection the author

58

Stix

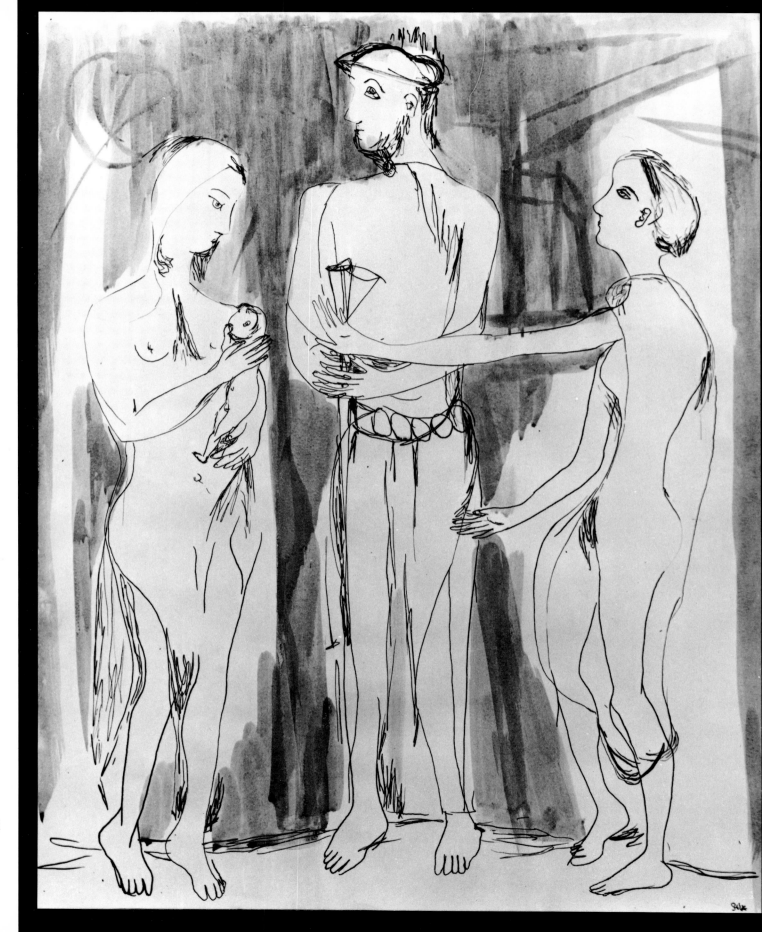

57 *The Rhine Maidens.* 1961. Ink, 22 x
   14". Washington Irving Gallery,
   New York City

58 *The Rhine Maidens.* 1961. Ink, 22 x
   14". Collection Theresa C. Brakeley,
   New York City

59 *The Judgment of Solomon.* 1960. Ink and
   wash, 24 x 19". Grand Rapids Art
   Museum, Grand Rapids, Michigan

60 *Cleopatra and the Asp.* 1962. Ink and
crayon, 24 x 19″. The William Benton
Museum of Art, University of
Connecticut, Storrs

61 *Cleopatra and the Asp.* 1962. Ink and felt
pen, 24 x 19″. Washington Irving
Gallery, New York City

62 *Apollo*. 1958. Ink, 18 x 24″. Collection
Hugh Stix, New York City

63 *Theseus and Ariadne*. 1960. Pencil, 16 x
11″. The William Benton Museum of
Art, University of Connecticut, Storrs

64 *Daphne*. 1961. Ink, 22 x 14″.
Washington Irving Gallery, New York
City

62 *Apollo.* 1958. Ink, 18 x 24″. Collection Hugh Stix, New York City

63 *Theseus and Ariadne.* 1960. Pencil, 16 x 11″. The William Benton Museum of Art, University of Connecticut, Storrs

64 *Daphne*. 1961. Ink, 22 x 14″.
Washington Irving Gallery, New York
City

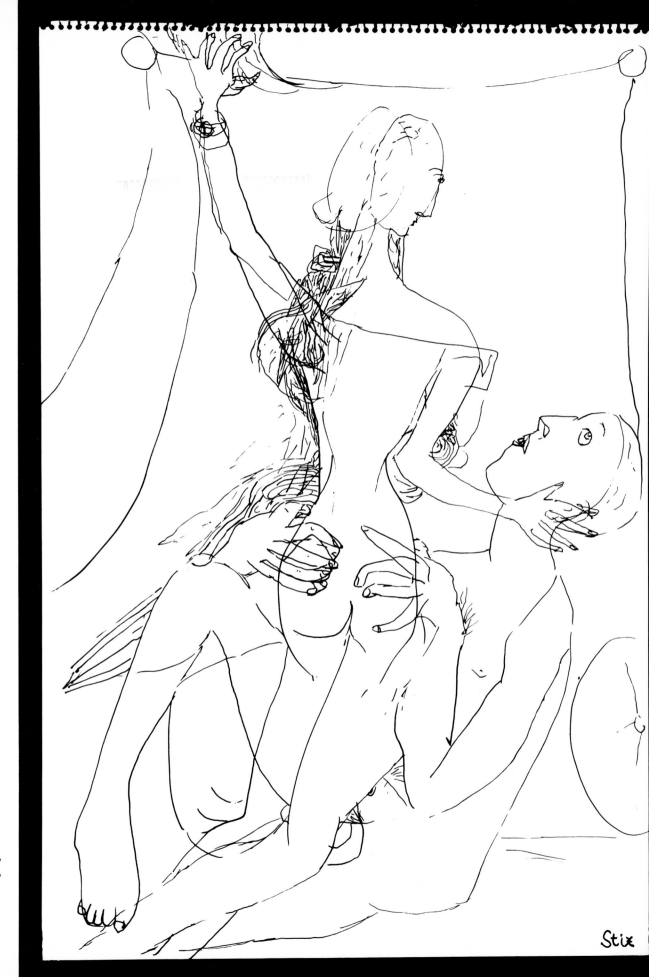

65 *Tamar Ravished by Ammon.* 1961. Ink,
   22 x 12". Washington Irving Gallery,
   New York City

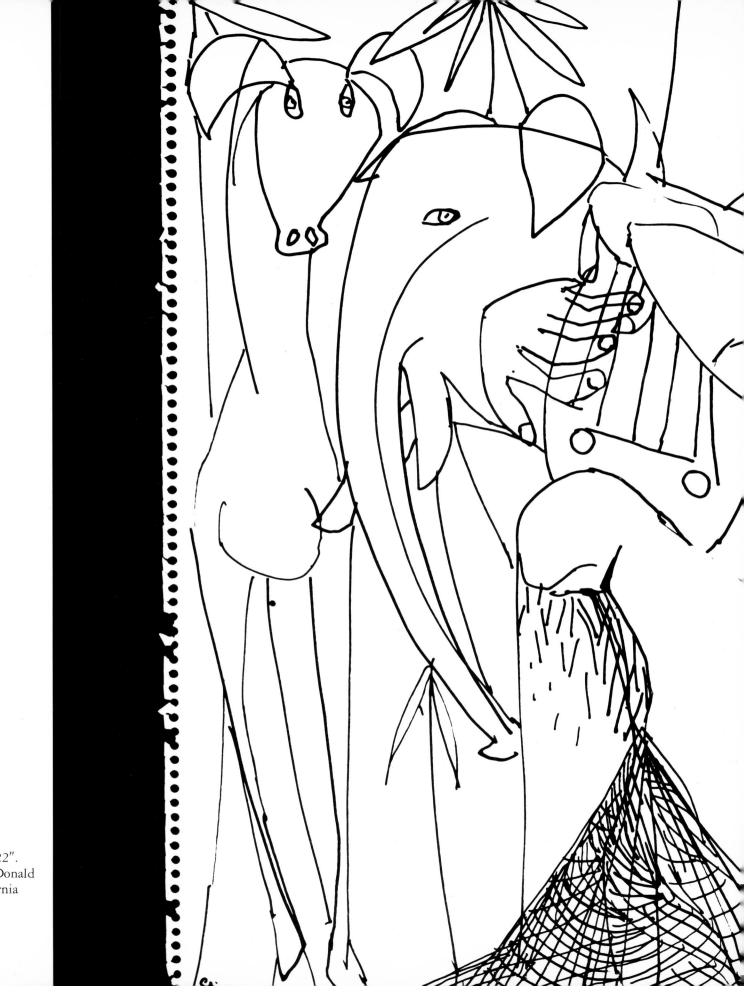

66 *Orpheus.* 1959. Ink, 14 x 22″.
Collection Mr. and Mrs. Donald
Graeber, Larkspur, California

Stix

67 *The Judgment of Paris.* 1961. Ink, 22 x
   14″. Minnesota Museum of Art,
   St. Paul

68 Detail of Plate 67

69

69 *Orpheus*. 1960. Pencil, 18 x 12".
Collection the author

70 *Europa*. 1958. Brown ink, 24 x 18".
Collection Robert Morton, Redding,
Connecticut

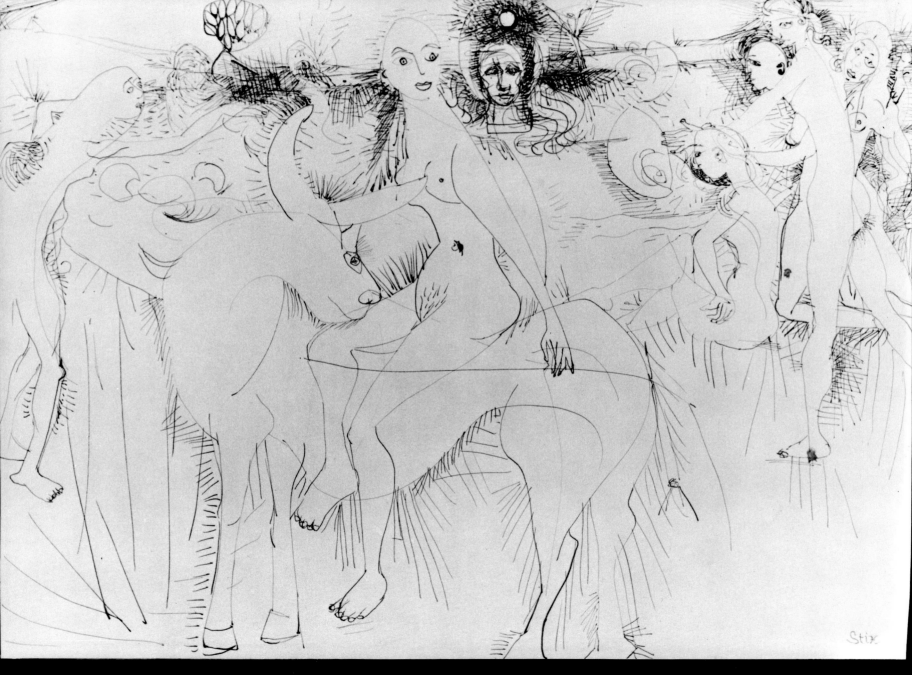

Stix

71 *Europa*. 1962. Ink, 11 x 8½".
Collection Emily S. Nathan,
New York City

sculptures

1949–1963

For some years Hugh Stix had been running The Artists' Gallery as an avocation, taking time from his business because of his interest in providing artists with a showcase that was not dependent upon either fashion or profit. For more than two decades it was a highly successful venture, presenting the work of those who would not otherwise have had the opportunity to exhibit. The Gallery's exhibitions received critical attention and developed a considerable following. It was there that such artists as Theodore Roszak, Ad Reinhardt, Adolph Gottlieb, Saul Baizerman, and Richard Pousette-Dart, among many others, got their start.

Marguerite first met Hugh Stix through The Artists' Gallery when, on the advice of friends, she made an appointment to show him her drawings from the concentration camp at Gurs, the only work that she had to present at the time. Though she never exhibited at the Gallery during its existence, she shared his belief in its purpose and his enthusiasm for its program, and she gave several benefits for it. Two were particularly memorable. "Paris in Greenwich Village" was the first, in December, 1949. She worked for two weeks in her own kitchen to put together a dinner for more than two hundred people. The menu, handwritten in Continental style, lists five hot and eight cold dishes, including "Choucroute à l'Alsacienne, Petit Vol-au-vent à la Financière, Anguilles au Vert à la Flâmande, Galantine de Canard Sauce aux Airelles," and a *pâté maison* and six choices for dessert. This was served throughout a long evening at a downstairs bar, while upstairs one could enjoy a selection of hot and cold sandwiches. A far cry from cooking whatever could be foraged for the Czech refugees in the remote mountains of southern France, this menu established that the culinary arts must be included among the others in which she excelled.

Thanks to the great success of the first, the second benefit, the following winter, had a still larger turnout, far too many for the MacDougal Street house. Marguerite rented the former Mori Restaurant on Bleecker Street, prepared a buffet in her kitchen, and took it to the restaurant on a pushcart borrowed from a friendly vegetable vendor. During the previous months she had become deeply interested in American jazz and had met a number of leading jazz musicians, among them Wilbur de Paris, president of the Jazz Guild of America. As a result, he and twenty-one others turned up to play for the benefit, including Cosy Cole, Buster Bailey, Willie "the Lion" Smith, Mary Lou Williams, George Wettling, and "Hot Lips" Page. For the more than three hundred who attended, it was another unforgettable experience. The fantastic decorations that Marguerite had made for the large room, and the food and drink, created an environment as stimulating to the musicians as to the other guests, who were treated to a series of remarkable performances that lasted until dawn.

In the meantime she was seriously pursuing sculpture, with small-scale works in terra cotta that she fired in a friend's kiln. By early 1951 she had accumulated enough pieces for a show, which opened at the Bertha Schaefer Gallery in December of that year. In this, her first exhibition in the United States, signing herself simply "Marguerite," she showed only terra cottas. They were unglazed, because she felt that glazing would distort the clean-cut, simplified forms, but she painted many of them in encaustic, maintaining a rather dry sculptural effect. Of the twenty-three pieces on exhibit, enough were sold so that she could turn from terra cotta to bronze, which became thereafter her favorite medium. The exhibition was well reviewed, and her American sculpture career was launched.

After this she worked directly in plaster and had casts made in small editions, usually numbering three or fewer. She did her own patination, so that there are often minor differences in color, tone, and value from one to another. She was fascinated with the entire procedure, and, as she later recalled, some of the happiest days of her life were spent at the Roman Bronze Foundry in Corona, Borough of Queens, New York. Because of her participation in each stage of the production, the results are more completely personal expressions and realizations of the artist's concepts than is usually the case. Here, as in all she did, her thorough knowledge of techniques was of great advantage. It gave her an assurance and control which were often the envy of others and which inform the resulting works, whether large or small. Well aware that importance has little relation to size, she showed in all her sculpture an unerring sense of the scale appropriate to the character of her own work.

There is a strong tendency toward reduction, toward abstraction, whatever the medium she adopted. In the terra cottas it shows itself in simplification of form, with figures (and often figures plus settings) ingeniously constructed according to the requirements of the ceramic medium. In the bronzes there is a greater tendency toward elongation, a nervously expressive surface, and the utilization of a transitional pose, a revealing stage in a continuing motion or sequence of events. The color, applied in encaustic or oil to the terra cottas, is the equivalent of the highly plastic treatment of the plasters to be cast in bronze, their surface rendered yet more individual by the patination that she manipulated at the foundry.

The years between 1949 and 1963 were devoted mainly to sculpture. The move from terra cotta to bronze in 1952 seems to have meant more than merely a change of medium. In Vienna Marguerite had worked freely in diverse materials on a large number of projects, including many commissions. Though in 1952–53 she produced a few pieces in alabaster, and from 1953 to 1955 experimented with balsa, mahogany, and ebony, from 1952 on she concentrated primarily on bronze. Its permanence and traditional quality appealed to her. It seemed the proper medium for the mature work which time and circumstance had forced her to defer until then. Within the next ten years she worked steadily, creating a body of sculpture of greater proportion than one would expect within that period, since she also found time for sketching and painting, including the numerous flower pieces, landscapes, the mythological drawings, and the Marilyn Monroe series.

The terra cottas displayed at the Schaefer Gallery in 1951 and the related woodcarvings show great sophistication in their almost toylike simplicity and a technical virtuosity that is not readily apparent, since each is complete and unitary, however complex the subject. These pieces create their own climate and atmosphere. They are so fully realized that one accepts, hardly noticing, a reflection in the terra-cotta mirror over the terra-cotta *Bar* with the figures grouped around it in a mood of quiet expectancy, as if awaiting someone, perhaps ourselves. In the same unlikely medium are the *Swimming Hole*, with its attendant figures and festive air, and the delightful *Nativity*, with its painted star. The arbitrary divisions required for firing the larger groups give no pause, so functionally, so frankly, but so adroitly are they made, and so integrally are the works composed. The feeling for the material, for its possibilities and limitations, seems instinctive, but the instinct is based upon knowledge acquired through extensive experience.

In these works there is often an enigmatic quality, as in *The Stairs*, with a reclining nude peacefully sleeping at the foot of a staircase curving upward into the unknown. Is the stair a figment of the dream of the sleeper? Does it lead to an escape, a wished-for experience, an ideal world we seek in dreams? And the *Trapped Figures*, struggling to free themselves from a tangle of impeding barriers and constricting forms, raise other and more disturbing questions.

There is a classic ease in the two groups entitled *Seated Woman with Child*, different though they are in detail; they are so serenely posed that the woman with the standing child inevitably suggests St. Anne with the infant Mary, while the one holding the baby in her lap could be the Virgin and Christ Child. In formal simplification the *Standing Nude* is clearly related, though the pose is curious, suggesting some inner tension.

Three figures in architectural settings show a subtle variety in mood: the *Atalanta*, colorfully garbed, alert, seated with a golden apple in one hand and a knife in the other, seen against a mythically blue sky; the *Seated Figure with a Bowl*, quiet and aware; and the nude *Half-reclining Figure*, relaxing with charming self-consciousness on a bench, with a window

72

73

72 *Nativity.* 1951. Painted terra cotta,
height 11″. Art Gallery, University of
Notre Dame, Notre Dame, Indiana

73 *Swimming Hole.* 1950. Painted terra
cotta, height 6″. Tennessee Botanical
Gardens and Fine Arts Center,
Nashville

and toilet objects nearby. In each the indication of surroundings and accessories, drastically simplified, as are the figures, has implications which extend beyond the given elements. The related *Susannah and the Elders* is in a sufficiently playful vein so that one does not worry too much about the girl's fate nor about the sinfulness of the soberly appreciative observers. The narrative aspect is so unobtrusively handled that it is no surprise to see the ease with which the sculptor presents two further Biblical compositions made up of many figures: the *Nativity* mentioned earlier and the *Descent from the Cross*. They are totally divergent in feeling, the first joyful, not only in the attitudes of the figures but also in the color, mainly blue and red; the second portentously grave, with the naturally somewhat austere surface of the terra cotta left untouched.

74

74 *The Bar.* 1951. Painted terra cotta, height 9". Minnesota Museum of Art, St. Paul

75 *The Stairs.* 1950. Painted terra cotta, height 8". Minnesota Museum of Art, St. Paul

75

76

76 *Atalanta.* 1950. Painted terra cotta,
   height 8″. Tennessee Botanical Gardens
   and Fine Arts Center, Nashville

77 *Man and Woman.* 1951. Painted terra
   cotta, height 5″. Minnesota Museum of
   Art, St. Paul

77

78

78 *Seated Woman with Child I.* 1950.
   Painted terra cotta, height 9″. Portland
   Museum of Art, Portland, Maine

79 *Seated Woman with Child II.* 1950.
   Painted terra cotta, height 10″.
   Minnesota Museum of Art, St. Paul

79

Several of the terra cottas display traits which seem transitional to the bronzes. In *Reclining Nude* and *Sleeping Nude* the forms are more deliberately modeled and constructed than is the case with many of the others, especially in the latter, which is almost cubistic in this regard. The hair is treated more nearly in the plaster-like style of the bronzes, and surfaces are more sculpturally handled. Something of the same is true of *Family Outing* also, which, in the rhythmic geometry of its composition, suggests the later bronze groups, though it retains a completely clayey feel in the cut-slab construction of the figures.

Whether in wood or stone, the shift in approach seems to have been effortlessly made from the building-up, modeling technique of both the terra cottas and the bronzes to the carver's technique of cutting away the superfluous to reveal the essential forms without destroying the sense of the original shape of the block out of which the figures are evoked. In the wood pieces color is used functionally: further to define form, as in *Eve* and *West Indian Market;* or further to unify it, as in the mahogany *Dancer,* whose painted decoration is reminiscent of the Vienna of Klimt, and whose pose suggests the figures illustrating the costume designs of Kolomon Moser or Léon Bakst. The *Nude Woman* seems both to emerge from and be bound by the ebony block from which it is carved with such apparent simplicity.

The bronzes are achieved with the same degree of technical knowledge, but with the shift of emphasis suitable to the more monumental medium. She handled the preliminary plasters with the same command, using texture to give liveliness to the surface. Form is again reduced to the basic, as in the terra cottas, but in terms of the more durable, less frangible material. Whereas the terra cottas are often made of sheets and rolls of clay, which preserve in the final fired and painted form a feeling of the malleability of the original material, the plasters are built up by swift daubs with the expressiveness and immediacy of brushstrokes translated into three dimensions.

The range of content and mood is greater in the bronzes, from the fluid upward thrust of *The Jump* and the ease and controlled grace of *Dancers* to the pathos of *Young Girl,* the *Self-portrait,* and the head of *Lincoln;* and from the fatigue and near despair of the *Seated Young Woman* to the youthful arrogance of *Anne on a Chair* and *Boy Leaning Against a Fence,* the gangling awkwardness of the *Girl on a Low Stool,* and the cocky showing off of the *Girl in a Rocking Chair.* The theme of mother and child occurs often among the bronzes also, as in *Bathing Group,* the maternal feeling of *Woman with a Child on Her Lap,* the tenderness of the *Woman with a Standing Child,* and the playful gesture and mutual enjoyment of the young

85 *Jazz I.* 1951. Painted terra cotta, height 10″. Minnesota Museum of Art, St. Paul

Mother and Infant. Greater emotional depth and expression tend to outweigh the charm with which Marguerite interpreted her subjects in bronze. The approach is more forthright, more uncompromising, and has more impact than in the other media.

The suggestion of the enigmatic comes through in the bronzes also: in the *Ascending Figure,* angular and taut with neurotic emotion; in the seated *Harriet* (a bronze-plated plaster), whose intense introspection is revealed not only by her facial expression but even more by the nervously interlaced fingers and the stiffly pointed toe; and in the hint of suffering conveyed by the *Girl Seated on the Floor.* There is also the same exploitation of the significant gesture, as in the upraised arms of the *Woman at Mirror,* in the quick turn of head of the *Girl with Poodle,* in the uneasy pulling at the collar of the *Seated Man,* in the stiff-armed pose of the *Leaning Woman,* and in the graceful motion of the *Woman Holding Slipper.*

Perhaps more closely related to her wood sculptures, in the search for simplified form while retaining a respect for the shape of the original material, are the pierced brass panels that Marguerite produced in the late 1950s. They combine a degree of distortion unusual for her (though it appears also in closely related contemporary drawings, such as the *Rhine Maiden* group) with a disregard of three-dimensional form which approaches a frontier of abstraction that is never actually crossed. The free linear pattern, etched in the surface, suggests something of the quality of certain primitive arts that she admired, perhaps of the Pacific islands.

Though many of Marguerite's sculptures are based on recollections of individuals seen in certain significant or revealing poses, her portrait sculptures fall into a separate category. They display a considerable range of subject and approach, from the early head of *Hugh Stix,* Despiau-like despite its almost orthodox realism, to the expressionistic and visionary *Lincoln,* of 1961, presented in that year by an anonymous donor to the New School for Social Research, where it is permanently installed in the library. Between 1951 and 1953 she was involved in a number of portrait projects, including the introspective *Nina Abrams* and the vivacious *Dede Pritzlaff,* both busts, and the half-lengths of her own *Self-portrait* and that of *Dorothea Weitzner,* all of which were exhibited at the Schaefer Gallery in December of 1953. The *Pritzlaff* bust was also shown at the Pennsylvania Academy the following year. There is, again, an echo of Despiau in the musing *Nina,* but in all four the rough treatment of the costume and the hair emphasizes the sensitivity of the modeling of the flesh, which also reveals the sculptor's awareness of the bone structure beneath. The hollowed eyes and parted lips give a sense of immediacy to the bust of *Dede,* and the almost distrait handling of the hair

86 *Woman and Child.* 1951. Painted terra cotta, height 13″. Collection Mrs. Edward Cafritz, Washington, D.C.

87 *Harlequin.* 1951. Painted terra cotta, height 14″. Private collection

86

87

suggests something of the troubled temperament underlying the vivacity that Marguerite found so attractive.

The seriousness, with a touch almost of sadness, of the expression of *Dorothea,* the poise of the head, and the sensitive modeling of the slender-fingered hands, held forward in a gesture of great delicacy, almost as if they were about to touch the keyboard of a musical instrument, make the bust perhaps the most appealing of all Marguerite's portraits. The lead, in which it is uniquely cast, seems, by its nature as well as by ancient association, to enhance ever so slightly the mood of gentle melancholy which pervades the sculpture.

By contrast, the head of *Harry Abrams* is almost masklike, and though competently and perceptively handled, it reveals comparatively little of the inner life of the sitter. There is more human content in the half-length *Portrait of Anne,* who was an unusually bright six-year-old, done while the child and her mother were visiting the Stixes in 1962. The little girl's precocious certainty and alertness are expressed in the life-size unique bronze.

Considered by the sculptor perhaps her outstanding work is the larger-than-life *Lincoln* head of 1961, mentioned above. It was inspired, like the two equestrian Lincolns, one of the same year and the other dating from 1962, by Carl Sandburg's biography and is based upon a number of contemporary likenesses—Brady photographs, daguerreotypes, and other sources—that Marguerite sought out, so deeply impressed was she with the extraordinary character revealed by the book. The later portrait of the president mounted, as Sandburg relates from a contemporary account, on a horse that seemed diminutive beneath Lincoln's gaunt height, is the last sculpture she did before turning to shells and jewelry in 1963. Its gesture of benediction is but another expression of the feeling that pervades the portrait head of two years before. In its quiet nobility and sadness the *Lincoln* head can stand as the climax of Marguerite's career in sculpture.

■

88 *Young Mother.* 1951. Terra cotta, height 13″. Collection Mrs. Susan Weisman, Scarsdale, New York

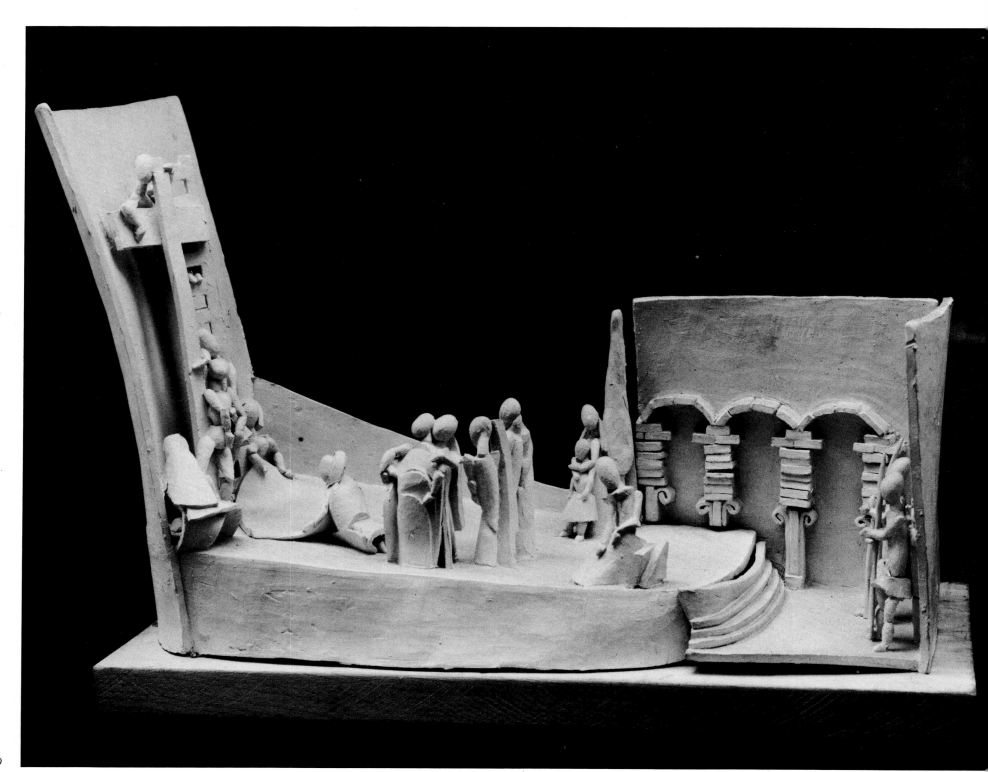

89

89 *Descent from the Cross.* 1951. Terra cotta,
height 13″. The Arkansas Art Center,
Little Rock

90 *Susannah and the Elders.* 1951. Painted
terra cotta, height 6½″. Collection
Mrs. Mary Tarcher, New York City

91 *Sleeping Nude.* 1952. Terra cotta, height
    4". Art Gallery, University of Notre
    Dame, Notre Dame, Indiana

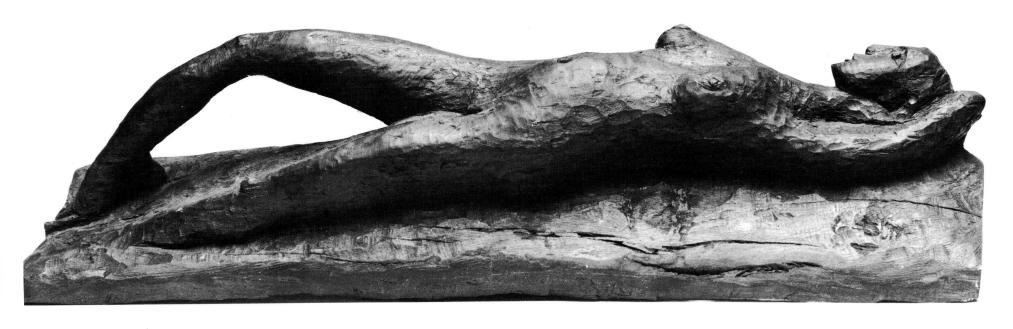

92 *Nude Woman*. 1954. Ebony, length
14". Portland Museum of Art,
Portland, Maine

93 *Reclining Nude.* 1952. Terra cotta,
height 9″. Minnesota Museum of Art,
St. Paul

94 *Torso.* 1953. Pink alabaster, height
11″. Minnesota Museum of Art,
St. Paul

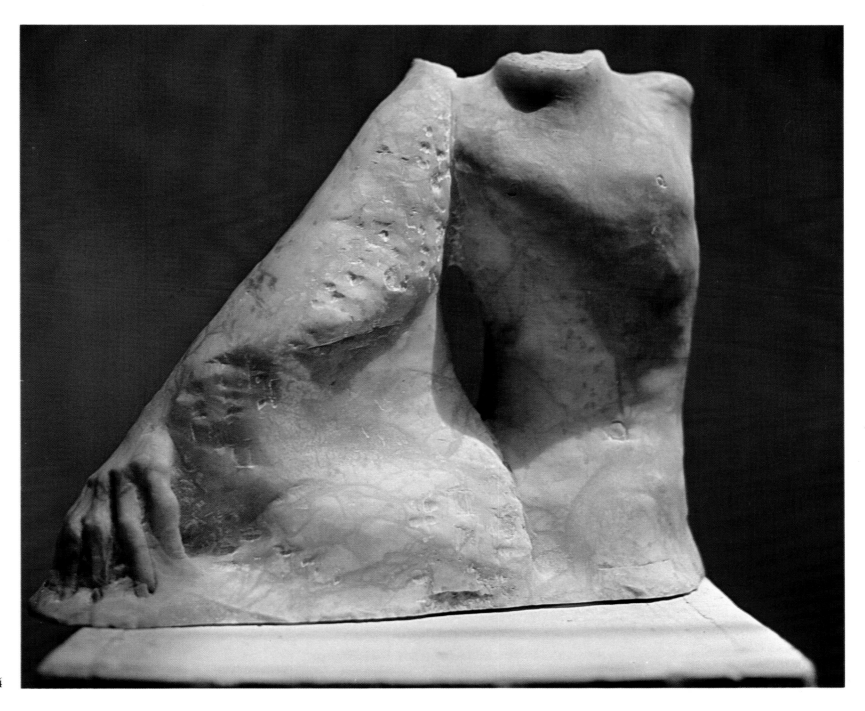

94

95 *Family Outing*. 1952. Painted terra
cotta, height 9″. Collection the author

96 Pierced brass reliefs. 1958. *Left:
Dancers*. Unique cast, height 28″.
Collection Dr. Max Colton, New York
City. *Right: Phaedra*. Unique cast,
height 45″. Philbrook Art Center,
Tulsa, Oklahoma

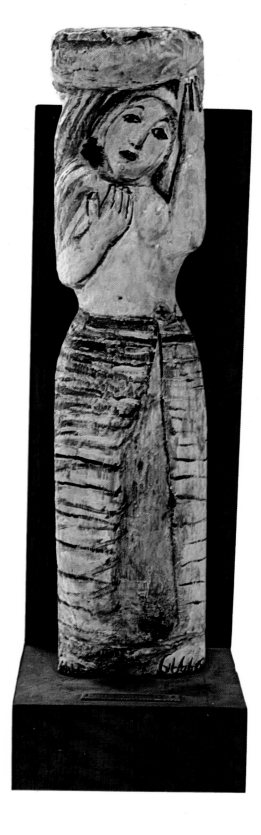

97

98

97 *Standing Woman*. 1952. Painted balsa, height 18″. Grand Rapids Art Museum, Grand Rapids, Michigan

98 *Eve*. 1954. Painted balsa, height 20″. Portland Museum of Art, Portland, Maine

99 *Dancer*. 1954. Painted mahogany, height 13″. Minnesota Museum of Art, St. Paul

100 *West Indian Market*. 1954. Painted balsa, height 22″. Des Moines Art Center, Des Moines, Iowa

99

100

101

101 *Seated Young Woman.* 1954. Bronze
(one of three), height 8″. Contemporary
Arts Museum, Houston, Texas

102 *Young Girl.* 1957. Bronze (one of four),
height 9½″. The Newark Museum,
Newark, New Jersey

103 *Young Woman on a Stool.* 1954. Bronze
(one of three), height 10″. Collection
Mrs. Alexander Salzman,
New York City

102   103

104

105

104 *Mother and Infant*. 1957. Bronze (one of
two), height 21″. Collection Mr. and
Mrs. J. M. Kaplan, New York City

105 *Bathing Group*. 1961. Bronze (one of
three), height 13″. Collection Gwen
Verdon, New York City

106 *Jamie and Nancy.* 1962. Bronze (unique cast), height 15″. Tennessee Botanical Gardens and Fine Arts Center, Nashville

107

107 *Girl on Horse.* 1956. Pencil, 24 x 19".
Washington Irving Gallery,
New York City

108 *Girl on Horse.* 1956. Carved balsa
original, height 45". (Bronze cast, one
of two, Raymond Burr Reading Room,
University of the Pacific, Sacramento,
California)

108

109 *Narcissus*. 1955. Bronze (one of two),
height 12″. Chrysler Museum of Art,
Norfolk, Virginia

110 *Kneeling Bather*. 1958. Bronze (one of
three), height 11″. Hirshhorn Museum
and Sculpture Garden, Washington,
D.C.

111 *Jazz II.* 1956. Bronze-plated plaster,
    height 12″. Minnesota Museum of Art,
    St. Paul

112 *Dancer Resting.* 1957. Bronze (one of
    three), height 20″. Walker Art Center,
    Minneapolis, Minnesota

112

113

114

113 *Self-portrait.* 1953. Plaster, height 52".
Minnesota Museum of Art, St. Paul

114 Bronze version (unique) of *Self-portrait.*
Plate 113. Wadsworth Atheneum,
Hartford, Connecticut

115 Alternate view of Plate 113

115

116

116 *Bust of a Woman (Portrait of Betti).*
1959. Bronze (unique cast), height 19″.
Washington Irving Gallery,
New York City

117 *Hugh's Mother.* 1954. Bronze (one of
two), height 13″. Collection Charlotte
L. Stix, Elmsford, New York

117

118 *Woman Seated on the Floor*. 1963. Bronze
(unique cast), height 19″. Art
Collection, University of Maine, Orono

119 *Girl with Poodle.* 1953. Bronze (one of
three), height 10″. Collection Mrs.
Clayton Dorn, Denver, Colorado

120

121

120 *Walking Woman*. 1958. Bronze (one of three), height 12″. Virginia Museum of Fine Arts, Richmond

121 *Anne on a Chair*. 1962. Bronze (unique cast), height 12″. Minnesota Museum of Art, St. Paul

122 *Paolo and Francesca*. 1958. Bronze (one of three), height 23″. The Columbia Museum of Art, Columbia, South Carolina

122

123

123 *Girl Seated on the Floor.* 1959. Bronze
(one of two), height 9″. Collection Fred
Harte, New York City

124 *Girl in a Rocking Chair.* 1960. Bronze
(one of two), height 11″. Minnesota
Museum of Art, St. Paul

124

125 *Horse.* 1959. Bronze (one of four), height 19″. Butler Institute of American Art, Youngstown, Ohio

126 *Newborn Donkey.* 1962. Bronze (one of six), height 12″. Collection Jerry Lewis, Hollywood, California

125

126

127 *Harriet.* 1959. Bronze-plated plaster, height 9″. Tennessee Botanical Gardens and Fine Arts Center, Nashville

128 *Infant.* 1959. Bronze (one of three),
height 9″. The Arkansas Art Center,
Little Rock

129 *Ballet*. 1960. Bronze (one of three),
    height 14″. Minnesota Museum of Art,
    St. Paul

130 Alternate view of Plate 129

131

132

131 *Dancers.* 1952. Bronze (one of two),
height 14″. Abrams Family Collection,
New York City

132 *The Jump.* 1957. Bronze (one of three),
height 13″. The Columbia Museum of
Art, Columbia, South Carolina

133 *Woman Holding Slipper.* 1959. Bronze
(one of three), height 15″. Collection
Mr. and Mrs. Meyer Mermin, New
Haven, Connecticut

133

134

134 *Woman with a Child on Her Lap.* 1959.
Bronze (one of three), height 16″.
Collection Mrs. Milton Weil, Sarasota,
Florida

135 *Woman at Mirror.* 1961–62. Bronze
(one of three), height 20″. Huntington
Galleries, Huntington, West Virginia

136 *Girl on a Low Stool.* 1959. Bronze (one
of three), height 13½″. Collection Mrs.
Albert List, New York City

135

136

137 - 138

137-138 *Portrait of Hugh Stix*. 1950. Bronze
(unique cast), height 18". Portland
Museum of Art, Portland, Maine

139 *Portrait of Harry Abrams*. 1956. Bronze
(unique cast), height 16". The William
Benton Museum of Art, University of
Connecticut, Storrs

139

141

140-142 *Portrait of Dorothea (Weitzner).* 1952.
Original plaster head (141) with gold
leaf, height 16″. Collection Margaret S.
Neilly, New York City. Alternate
views of half-length version (140, 142).
Lead (unique cast), height 31″.
Philbrook Art Center, Tulsa,
Oklahoma

143 *Portrait of Nina Abrams.* 1953. Bronze
(unique cast), height 26″. Abrams
Family Collection, New York City.
Plaster version, The William Benton
Museum of Art, University of
Connecticut, Storrs

144 *Portrait of Dede Pritzlaff.* 1952.
Original plaster, height 28″. Tennessee
Botanical Gardens and Fine Arts
Center, Nashville. Bronze (unique
cast), Collection Mrs. Edward F.
Pritzlaff, Hartland, Wisconsin

145 *Woman with a Standing Child.* 1959.
Bronze (one of three), height 12″.
Minnesota Museum of Art, St. Paul

146 *Family Group.* 1962. Bronze (one of
two), height 16″. Minnesota Museum
of Art, St. Paul

146

147

147   *Equestrian Lincoln I.* 1962. Bronze
       (unique cast), height 25″. Des
       Moines Art Center, Des Moines,
       Iowa

148-149 *Lincoln.* 1959. Bronze (two of three),
       height 23″. The New School for Social
       Research, New York City. Also The
       William Benton Museum of Art,
       University of Connecticut, Storrs

148 - 149

150 *Equestrian Lincoln.* 1963. Bronze (one of two), height 24″. Tennessee Botanical Gardens and Fine Arts Center, Nashville

shells and jewelry

1963—1974

151 Marguerite showing her fabric design with shell motifs, 13 Vandam Street, 1971

Late in January, 1963, the firm with which Hugh Stix had been associated during all his business life was sold, and unexpectedly he found himself without commitments. "Wonderful!" was Marguerite's reaction. "At last we can do something together!" Without a sign of regret, she gave up her sculpture career, though she continued to show her work at the Washington Irving Gallery.

The joint venture on which she and Hugh decided was something which had long fascinated her: seashells, which she had regarded all her life as objects of great beauty. In the introduction to their book, *The Shell: Five Hundred Million Years of Inspired Design* (1968), she expressed their aim: "We wanted . . . to restore some of the admiring awe man had experienced throughout history for the work of these strange sea creatures, master builders whose architectural miracles embodied the bases of a multitude of mathematically correct vaults, arches, staircases, porticoes, and niches. We wanted to direct attention to a world of ideas that might give fresh meaning and stimulation to the contemporary arts—to free-form creation, sculpture, architecture, design—especially to those areas where confusion and darkness seem to prevail. . . . We decided we would search the world for the most beautiful and glamorous shells we could find and exhibit them in a simple but elegant way as objects deserving attention and respect."[7]

In the summer of 1963 the Stixes went on a trip to the main shell-producing areas of the Pacific. After visiting Tokyo and Kyoto, they went to Hong Kong, the Philippines, Australia, New Zealand, the Fijis, the Solomons, Tahiti, and Hawaii and returned to New York with some fifteen thousand specimens. It was in Japan that Marguerite began to have a still deeper feeling for the subject. They visited a number of the leading Japanese collectors, whose knowledge and sophisticated, almost mystical appreciation especially impressed them. "We shall never forget," she later wrote, "visiting the house of a notable collector-scientist in Kyoto. . . . We knelt . . . on the matted floor, . . . a company of four brought together by a common interest. . . . Certain rare shells were delicately lifted from their boxes by our host and placed on a low table before us. . . . Conversation . . . ceased. . . . The atmosphere, beginning in a relaxed mood, had . . . become ceremonial."

To understand shells better, Marguerite began a series of drawings of them, working with a sustained, fluent line at large scale to capture the details of form and pattern. When Theodore Rousseau, Jr., then Curator of European Painting at the Metropolitan Museum, first saw the series, he exclaimed, "I don't know of another artist of our times but Matisse whose drawings can compare with these!" Marguerite later made lithographs of shells in the same flowing line and, later still, based striking fabric and wallpaper designs on them.

152

152 *Epitonium scalare.* 1964. Ink, 24 x 18″.
   Delaware Museum of Natural History,
   Greenville

153 *Harpa davidis.* 1964. Ink, 24 x 18″.
   Delaware Museum of Natural History,
   Greenville

154 *Cymatium lotarium.* 1964. Ink, 24 x
   18″. Delaware Museum of Natural
   History, Greenville

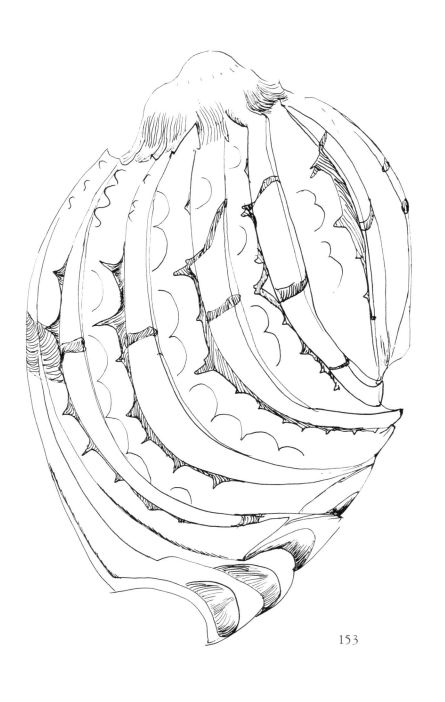

153

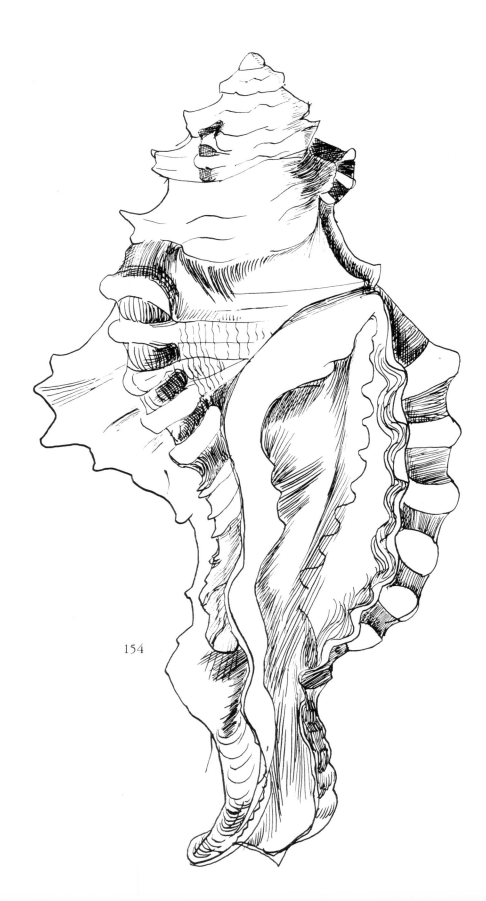

154

155 Marguerite working in her studio, 13 Vandam Street, 1974

156 The Stix Stand designed and patented by Marguerite, 1964

While working on these drawings, she designed a slender, crescent-shaped metal stand to hold the shells upright so that she could study them better. The stands were so successful that shell collectors everywhere insisted on having them. She took out a patent on the design and found craftsmen to produce it in quantity. The Stix stand, which started out as a simple convenience for the artist, is now known worldwide and has been much imitated, as has the three-footed ring that she developed as a support for larger shells.

The first exhibition of shells took place on March 1, 1964. For the occasion Marguerite had transformed the drawing room of the house on Vandam Street (to which the Stixes had moved in 1956) into a gallery, and she served *coquilles St.-Jacques* to those invited to the opening. It was attended, as she wrote later, "by friends, artists, and the press, and the initial enthusiasm of this small group made itself felt at once in ever-widening circles." The presentation of the shells was beautifully done and the timing perfect. Within days there was recognition in newspapers and on television and, later, with illustrations in color, in magazines. Shells began to appear everywhere—in advertisements, fashion photographs, shop windows—as design motives. All sorts of people sought out the house on Vandam Street, which became a meeting place (or, in the words of one frequent visitor, a prominent designer, "an oasis") for all who shared the Stixes' fascination.

A great part of the success of Marguerite's installation was to present the shells as works of art, as found objects of extraordinary interest. As she wrote in *The Shell,* "We have tried . . . to let the shells speak for themselves in their own language." In retrospect the book seems an almost inevitable development. "Because of the enthusiasm generated by our modest beginning," she wrote, "we believe that there is a corresponding reservoir of enthusiasm that can be reached only through the medium of the book." The publication has gone through many printings and foreign-language translations, and a paperback version was issued in 1972. Her aim, to share her delight in the subject, has been realized; thousands of readers have entered the same "world of enchantment" that she found.

The text of *The Shell* is credited in the book to Hugh and Marguerite Stix, because she wished especially to emphasize that theirs was a joint venture. According to her husband, however, she herself wrote the entire introduction in three days, bringing together in her charming and thoughtful essay the results of months of research and study. Hugh then edited her text, for English was not her native tongue, though she spoke it fluently. The scientific data, the identifications, and the illustration captions were then checked by the distinguished malacologist R. Tucker Abbott.

When Marguerite began studying shells in detail, she considered them first as abstract sculptures and then, recalling her experience in Vienna and Paris (where she had designed and produced unique fashion accessories in ceramics and metal), as potential elements of jewelry, as gems equivalent in their own way to precious stones. Beginning with a brooch made of a single shell with a metal pin, she went on to design necklaces, bracelets, pendants, rings, earrings, belt buckles—all sorts of jewelry. The rings she made from mitered sections of the black-and-white marble cone and other strongly patterned shells, set in gold or silver, with red, black, white, or green enamel, became for many a symbol of elegance, as recognizable as an autograph. Small bivalves of differing colors and univalves tipped at their points with stones became rings and earrings. Harking back to her sculpture, she still made some pieces of cast gold in figural form, but most of her jewelry involved combinations of shells in metal settings, with or without gemstones.

Baroque pearls, whose irregular shapes often make them surprising examples of organic form in miniature scale, were particularly attractive to Marguerite. She also recognized the quality of pale emeralds, usually disregarded by jewelers, and, as a result of her example, both baroque pearls and pale emeralds, which previously had been scarcely salable, suddenly became fashionable. She reinforced the delicate edges and apexes of shells with precious metals, much as Renaissance goldsmiths did with nautilus and other shells to create splendid objects for their noble, royal, and ecclesiastical patrons. The natural hinges of bivalves she replaced with hinged mounts in silver or gold to make pillboxes, lockets, or watch cases. She made evening cases from nautilus shells and mounted large shells of the scallop family on sculptured bases in the form of mermaids cast in gold or silver and encrusted with tiny shells and pearls.

In all the designs shells are the primary elements, but they are accompanied and enhanced by pearls, emeralds, rubies, amethysts, sapphires, opals, and other stones in the settings of gold or silver. Form, color, and texture are carefully coordinated. The pieces are always composed with simplicity and elegance and made up with unusual juxtapositions. A flame-augur pendant, for example, is suspended from a necklace of tubular turquoise beads interspersed with carnelian and gold orbicles; a cone with a tapestry-like pattern of dull orange hangs from a chain of baroque pearls and granulated gold cylinders; a volute with a sinuous linear design is the pendant of a string of chalcedony and amethyst beads spaced with mat gold cylinders and accented with a roseate tourmaline; or a collar of thin gold is set with silvery, opaline shells, pale tourmalines, and a pale emerald. The intervals and placement of

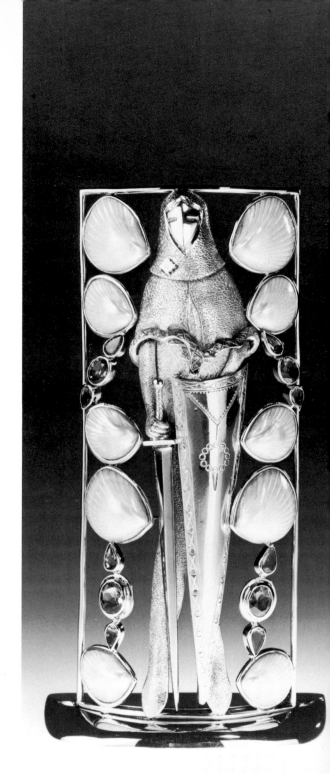

157

these elements are as important as the massing, and, despite their richness, the effect is one of lightness and understatement.

The shells and pearls enhance the liquid quality of the transparent or translucent stones and the soft sheen of metals to suggest in many pieces the cool nacreous glow of a Nereid world. Others, stronger in color and more robust in design, carry implications of Egyptian, Byzantine, medieval, or Renaissance precedent; yet none is derivative; all have an unqualified originality. The historical inferences are a measure of Marguerite's awareness of the past, a past that she studied with dedicated interest and to which she turned often for inspiration but never tried to copy or to emulate.

Though she frequently used stones of the finest quality in her jewelry, it was the essential beauty rather than the monetary value or the rarity of the various elements that mattered to her. With uncommon sensitivity, by means of design that is seemingly simple yet often of great subtlety, she composed her diverse materials into pieces of originality, variety, and distinction, realized with impeccable craftsmanship. The result was to raise the jeweler's craft once again to the realm of art, as in the best of the works created in the great tradition of the past.

To the fulfillment of this aim she brought all the knowledge of her Viennese years, of the Wiener Werkstätte philosophy of design, of the achievements in this and related fields of Wagner, Moser, Hoffmann, and many others, including Carl Otto Czeschka, a designer and goldsmith who had taught in the Kunstgewerbeschule and produced, early in this century, distinctive jewelry emphasizing, above all, excellence in design and workmanship. Her study in museums, from Vienna to Paris, London, and finally New York, was immensely useful. And, as her husband later wrote, "The frustration of not being able to continue her

157 *King Arthur.* 1973. Shells, gold, silver, emeralds, and tourmalines, height 6". Commissioned by Gabriel Lucas Limitée, Montreal

158 Marguerite preparing for Cartier exhibition, May, 1972

31 Jan. 1972

for pendant,   Pin-pendant
ring hidden
in back

OPAL

large
Nautilus-pearl

oval ivory
back

malachite cab
oval slender
coral

small
nacre pearl

amethyst cab.

small naut
pearl

small
nautilus
pearl

amethyst cab

large coral cab.

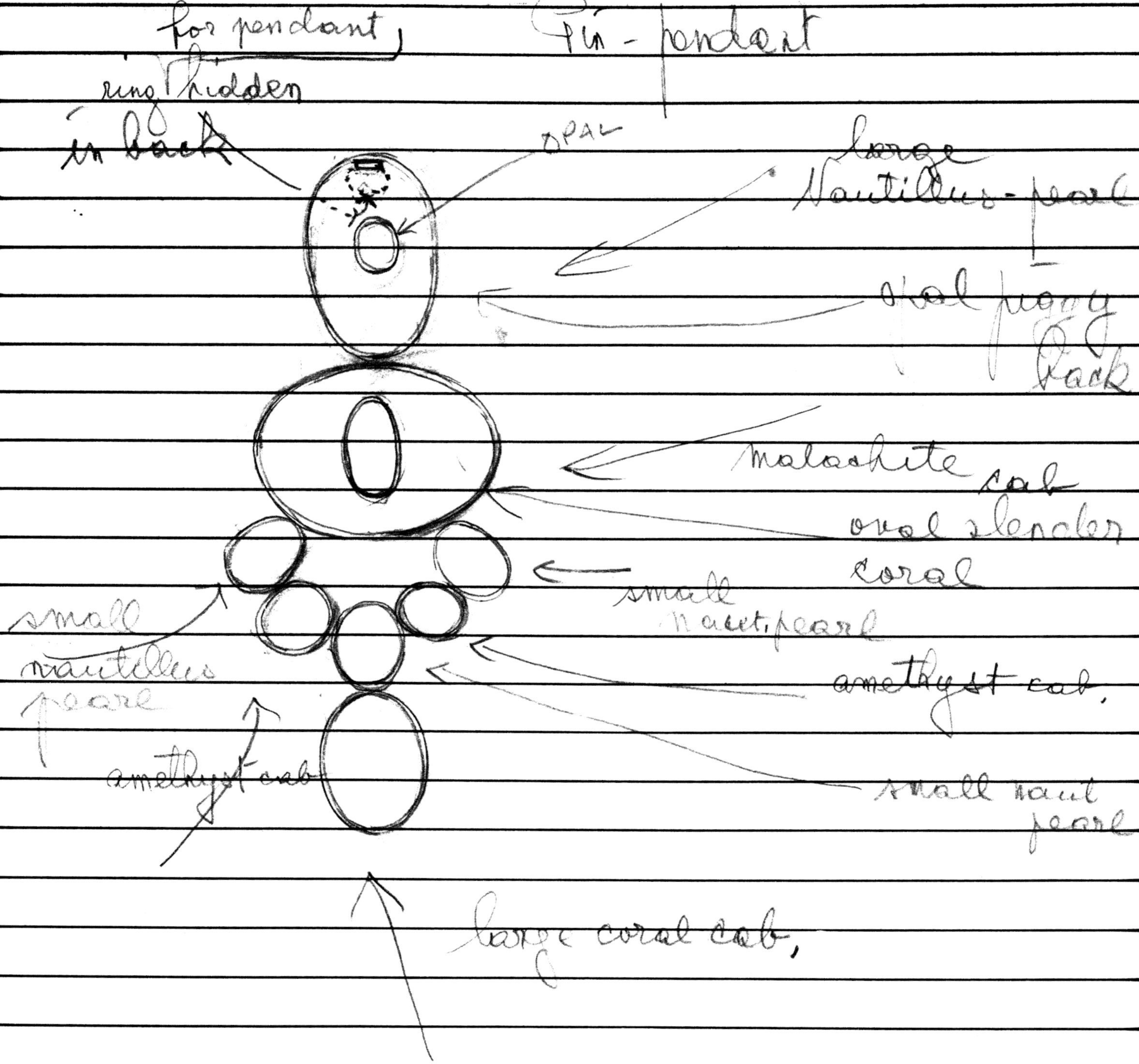

A.D. 501

beloved bronze sculpture poured into these myriad exquisite works of art." She planned each piece with great care, paying attention to such considerations as how certain shells would hang as pendants, how bracelets and necklaces would perform when worn.

She found craftsmen in France, Italy, Spain, Portugal, and the United States to carry out her designs according to her detailed drawings and precise directions, each idea being minutely worked out at first by herself. She modeled and carved her own waxes for the gold caster and determined the position of each element of each piece in drawings made to full scale. Many jewelers and goldsmiths told her that she was asking the impossible at times, but she found solutions, no matter how much time and effort were involved, and even the most difficult pieces were eventually made as she had planned, to the admiration of those who worked with her. Consequently, she could count on the highest standard of workmanship on the part of all who executed her projects, since they recognized in her not only an artist but also a skilled fellow craftsman, whose appreciation and respect they valued.

The same creative energy and discipline that she brought to all her endeavors were applied to the Stixes' shell program, and with notable results. Their book, *The Shell,* became a continuing best-seller, and her jewelry and other objects made with shells set a standard of fashion and quality that received international notice. Her work was selected for official presidential giving, appeared frequently in leading magazines, and entered private and museum collections. Yet, despite the ever-increasing demand, she avoided repetition and maintained the same exacting criteria, so that every piece is unique. She was always on the lookout for outstanding examples of shells, whether rare or common. Each was studied individually, with the idea of using it, either alone or in combination with others, in the way best suited to emphasize its particular characteristics of form and color. Her respect for the object is shown by the care she took always to present the shells so that they "speak for themselves in their own language."

The fame of the jewelry and other shell pieces tended to overshadow Marguerite's accomplishments as a sculptor and a painter, yet the designs always show her sculptor's sense of three-dimensionality and significant form, while the subtlety and range of the color schemes equally prove her painter's eye. In its blending of vigor and refinement, of diversity and consistent quality, the jewelry deserves consideration with her other work as yet another expression of an unusual and versatile creative gift.

■

159 Working drawing for a pin-pendant, with nautilus pearls, opal, malachite, coral, and amethyst. 1972

160 Pin-pendant developed from working drawing, Plate 159

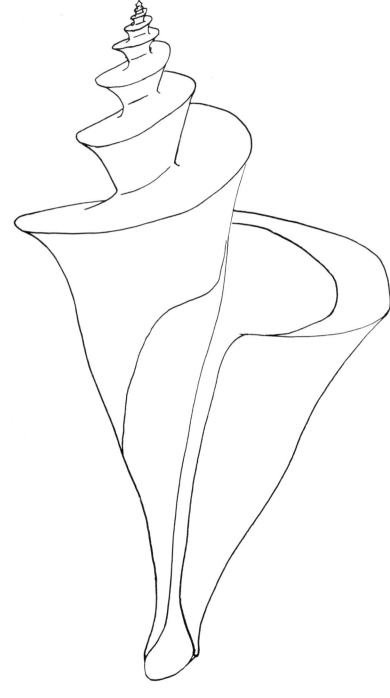

161

161 Freestanding white shell stabile. 1964.
Assemblage, 12 x 18″. Rare Shells, Inc.,
Palm Beach, Florida

162 *Thatcheria mirabilis*. 1964. Ink, 24 x
18″. Delaware Museum of Natural
History, Greenville

Lion's Paw Shell Box. 1970. 18-carat gold and shell, with clasp of gold cast from a rare coral flower centered on a fire opal. The Headley Museum, Lexington, Kentucky

Pin-pendant-necklace. 1973. Shells, gold, rubies, emeralds, and baroque pearls

Unicorn Pin. 1970. Gold, shell, and garnets

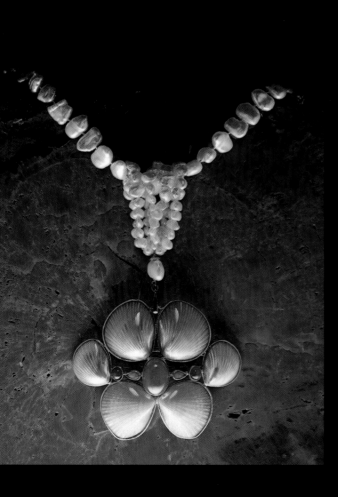

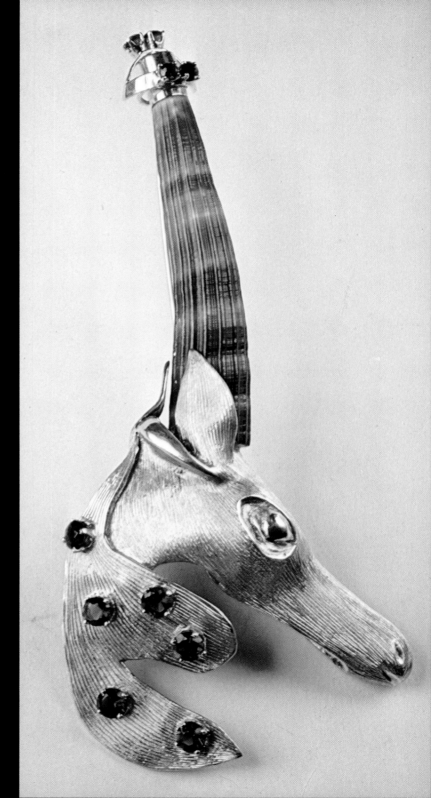

165

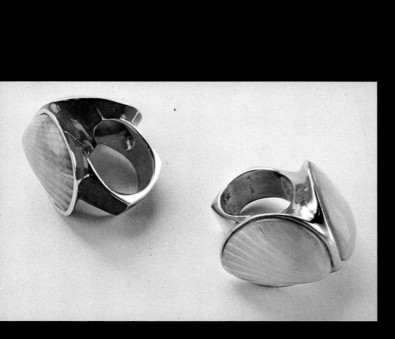

Two versions of Marguerite's most famous
ring, the *Margaretacea*, 1965

169 *Moonshot Ring*. 1970. Gold, shell, and
gemstone

171

173

170 Paper knives. 1967. Shell, vermeil,
malachite, and lapis

171 Shell case for watch. 1969. Gold and
shell with amethyst chatelaine

172 Clip. 1970. Shell, gold, ruby, and
emeralds

173 *Mermaid.* 1970. Vermeil and shells.
Collection Louis J. Gartner, Palm
Beach, Florida

Eton collar. 1969. Gold, shell,
tourmaline, and aquamarine

176 Collar. 1970. Shells, gold, and
emeralds

Bracelet. 1970. Nautilus pearls, gold,
turquoise, and tortoise shell

178 Necklace. 1971. Shell, coral, and jade

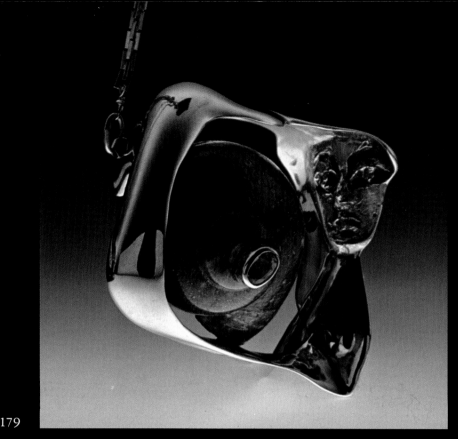

179

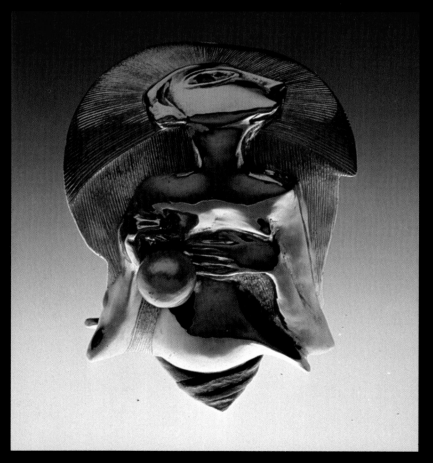

180

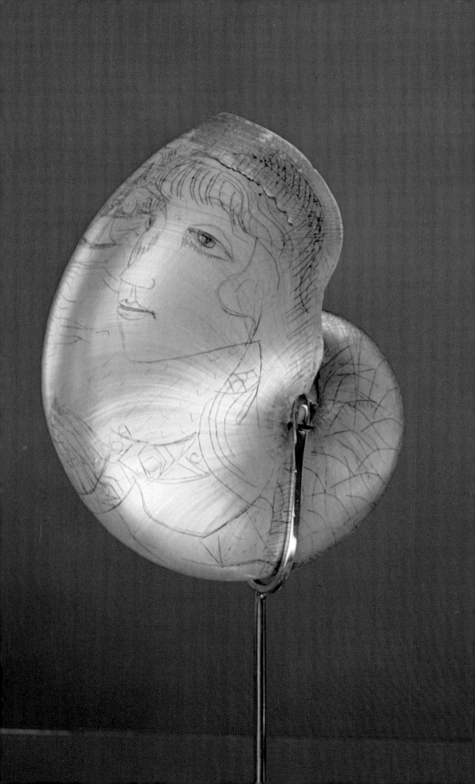

her inner world

The artistic career of Marguerite Stix was identical to her personal life in that, in any circumstance (and there were many disruptive events beyond her control), she met each crisis positively and imaginatively. Her attitude toward life was consistently constructive, just as it was consistently craftsmanlike in the realization of her creative impulse. Everything she did was, to her, infinitely worth the doing and was executed with style and grace. At the same time there was a power, as well as originality, in her output, and the whole was illuminated by a capacity for human relations based upon appreciation and respect that were deeply discerning but not uncritical.

Even with the gifts which were the result of a happy combination of genes, she was fortunate in the place and the time of her birth—Vienna in the early decades of this century, as described earlier. Fully aware of her good luck in growing up and studying in the city of Hoffmann, Loos, Klimt, and Schiele, she pursued her career, in whatever medium served best at the time and under the prevailing circumstances, with the conviction that she shared a vital tradition and, in her own particular way, was one of its continuators.

A great deal of development had gone on during the years when she had not been able to work as an artist. Her approach to form had changed from an essentially romantic, idealistic, and stylized interpretation of representation to a more rigorous system of conceptualization—more abstract, more individual, more expressive—with a correspondingly greater mastery of technique, governed by a maturing of perception. Her capacity to grow, to turn adversity into creative enrichment, was, perhaps, her outstanding accomplishment as a person and as an artist.

Increasingly she worked toward reduction of means to gain freer expression. Increasingly the significant gesture came to stand for the whole, in all its complexity of implication. Here her lifelong interest in the theater played a part in the evolution of her sculptural style. The rhythms of her work often reflected equally her love of music and the dance. Classical music was a vital element from early childhood. Also, she came to be fascinated with jazz, and classical Spanish guitar held a special appeal for her. The control and coordination of the dancer were hers, for the study of voice and dance during her teens had not only deepened her musical understanding but also brought together basic aspects of the theatrical and musical worlds so that they became a permanent influence on her emotional and intellectual life. Her paintings and sculptures have something of the nature of the performance about them, while her drawings particularly take on the improvisational

183 *Jazz III*. 1956. Bronze (one of two),
   length 19″. Butler Institute of
   American Art, Youngstown, Ohio

qualities of jazz. In both painting and drawing, and to a lesser extent in sculpture, her work deals frequently with variations on themes in a manner directly comparable to music. One has merely to consider the flower pieces and the Marilyn Monroe series for examples.

Marguerite's love for the primitive arts in various areas of the world, from archaic Greece to Polynesia, broadened her three-dimensional imagery. In the terra cottas there are hints of the early Greek and Minoan, of Mohenjo-Daro and Central America, of clay figurines from Egyptian tombs and Mesopotamian excavations. Little is visible of Rodin, whose works she knew well, or of Bourdelle, his pupil, in whose studio she had studied, nor much of Despiau, whose reserve and basic classicism were compatible with her temperament. There are only remote and occasional echoes of the Viennese art styles with which she was so familiar during her formative and student years. The lessons were well learned. For one of her period, background, and education, she was always unusually independent and self-reliant in anything she undertook.

184 Marguerite at work on *Jazz III,* 1956

185 The ceramic studio and workshop at 134 MacDougal Street, Christmas, 1948

186 Collection of Christmas angels made over the years for friends. Various media. Minnesota Museum of Art, St. Paul

The unusual breadth of practical knowledge and the basic principles gained through her association with Hoffman and the Wiener Werkstätte served Marguerite well throughout her entire subsequent life. The idea that all aspects of life are a proper arena for the creative spirit, that no human activity is alien to the designer's sensitivity, from cooking to sculpture, was completely sympathetic to her. The Christmas angels she made for friends each year—some of painted Chianti bottles, some of marzipan, some of terra cotta—ephemeral or not, received the same inventive and skillful attention as her other work. She arranged hors d'oeuvres like fantastic abstract sculptures and painted linoleum in her own adaptation of Delft tiles. She molded the physical environment in which she lived, regardless of its material limitations, to her own aesthetic specifications, as an outward manifestation of her inner world. Yet her innate scale of values remained intact, allowing of no confusion among the various areas of her endeavor. For her, with a rare clarity, art was, indeed, a function of life.

187

188

187   Christmas angels made from Chianti
bottles for friends, MacDougal Street,
Christmas, 1948

188-189   Christmas cookies made for friends,
MacDougal Street, 1947

190-191   Marguerite creating abstract sculpture
with hors d'oeuvres

189

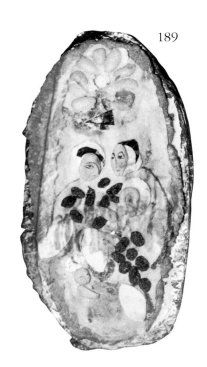

190-191

Her essentially humanistic view of life, and of art, was demonstrated by the growing preoccupation in her work with the human condition. In this respect she followed time-honored traditions, not through default nor because of a necessity to cling to the recognizable for reasons of security, but because of a sense of conviction annealed by circumstance into a philosophy that was to carry through her later life and her mature work. Whereas the spirit of others had been blighted by similar adversities, hers, buttressed by the

192

193

194

192 Buttons and pins. 1943–48. Ceramic. Minnesota Museum of Art, St. Paul, and Cooper-Hewitt Museum, New York City

193 Necklace. 1947. Ceramic. Minnesota Museum of Art, St. Paul

194 Enamel on silver for use in pins. 1948. Minnesota Museum of Art, St. Paul

inherent strength and faith derived from the solid background of her early years, was sustained. It became ever more natural for her to realize her concepts in basic human statements. In the light of her personal history, it is easy to understand her celebration of the beautiful in the series of watercolors, oils, and pastels of flowers, of landscapes, of the wonders of every day. Gratitude for survival and an enhanced joy in living are not only reflected but also clearly expressed in all her work, which is, in essence, an affirmation of life. It could not be anything else but objective and largely figural, since the feeling of shared humanity is strengthened in one who has come close to losing life itself.

Despite the outward ease with which she appears to have surmounted disasters and carried out her work, she had a pitch of inner sensibility which emerges most notably in her self-portraits and drawings, though its traces appear in much of her other art. The drawings, especially, skirt the bounds of the nonobjective as they probe the dreamlike but disturbingly proximate world of subconscious feelings and desires. The vehicle is usually the traditional mythic matter of classical or Biblical inheritance, but its effectiveness reflects the completeness with which she assimilated that inheritance to make it a language of her own.

A sense of intimacy pervades her work. It is expressed by a consistent moderateness of scale, which she maintained throughout and is a function of her artistic integrity. With the security of thoughtful dedication, varied experience, and intelligence, and with a continuing fascination with art in all its manifestations and an acute sense of the natural world and man's relation to it, she found no need for parade. Understatement better suited her temperament, her understanding, and the strict discipline she brought to every aspect of her life. It intensified her tendency to the use of the visual metaphor and provided a high degree of freedom to range broadly within a chosen scope and according to self-imposed limits.

The vividness of her inner life is revealed by many facets of her work. Much more is suggested than stated, however. Her art is very personal, not only in style and symbol but also in its reticent, almost secretive character. She gives us momentary visions of her private world in the brilliance of the flower pieces, in the acuity of her observations of nature and her special response to it. But these are glimpses, nothing more. The enigmatic quality of a number of her sculptures and many of her drawings adumbrates the complexity and variety of that inner environment but never fully unveils it, merely intimating some of its dimensions. It was this world, created during a lonely childhood, peopled by history and myth, structured by her exceptional early training and associations, which offered a psychological refuge when she was imprisoned at Gurs and gave her the power and resource to succeed in the various creative fields she entered. Study, observation, reading, and experience enriched that world throughout her life, yet her practicality and sense of the immediate never allowed it to become merely an escape. It is there that her gaze is directed in her self-portraits, which look at us but beyond us into an otherwhere, the milieu in which she lived her creative life and from which came her art. With all the diversity of artistic expression she left behind, its integrity and its mystery remain.

In the spirit that runs through her work she was very much a denizen of the post-Freudian era, aware of its wracking doubts and of the raw frontiers opened suddenly into the inner space of the subconscious, of hitherto largely unexplored motivations and emotions. In much that she did she sought to express inner life by outward means, to reveal the significance of a pose, a gesture, a glance by suggesting its transcendent implications. Her sculptured portraits are examples of this, especially the *Dorothea* and her own *Self-portrait*. In the latter, the turned and slightly tilted pose of the head, the large, thoughtful eyes, the parted lips, the attenuation of the neck and torso, the delicacy of the hands in their almost hesitant gesture, and the slenderness of the arms all combine to create the meditative air of the whole. The feeling is more withdrawn than in the bust of *Dorothea*. Despite the vulnerability, there is a certain reserve, a privacy, about it, and the solitariness of one who has undergone much and has much to remember. More than all the others, this is an attempt directly to portray the inner being.

The series of drawn and painted self-portraits make clear that the artist saw herself in many different moods and as revealing multifarious traits of personality. In the bronze, she seems to have successfully created a unified whole, suggestive, nonetheless, of the variety of feeling within. Whether she was aware of it at the time or not, the little red terra-cotta head of 1950–51, exhibited as *Head of a Woman* in the Schaefer Gallery exhibition of 1953, may well represent a preliminary study for the *Self-portrait*. which was first shown at the same time. The tilt of the head, the large, emotional eyes, and the delicate parted lips, as well as the hair treatment and overall slenderness, are very close to the larger sculpture both in form and in mood.

Unlike much art of recent times, Marguerite's shows no chic theorizing, no playing with form and concept such as can be done only in a situation of nearly total security and remoteness from life. In spite of her innate reserve, the vigor of her works discloses the intensity of her feeling for life, for people, for human situations, and for her awareness of herself, no matter how figuratively or allusively expressed. The translation of that feeling

195 *Head of a Woman*. 1950–51. Red terra
cotta, height 6″. Minnesota Museum of
Art, St. Paul

into form, both two-dimensional and three-, was her constant aim. The immediacy comes
through. In looking at her works, whatever the medium, we instinctively share her
priorities. The result is, in Berenson's phrase, "life-enhancing."

If there is a single key to Marguerite's life, it may be found in a passage near the end of
her account of the concentration camp, where all the prisoners suffered even more than the
miserable circumstances demanded through being allowed nothing to do. "Work would
have meant much more than only occupation," she wrote. "Work is creative. It is a power
leading to faith again."[2] After that experience her faith, upheld by work, never faltered.
Again and again, under all sorts of difficulties, she drew on the sustenance of her years in
Vienna, where she had learned to believe that everything can be viewed creatively, that to
every problem the only real hope for solution lies within the realm of the artist's imagination.
Perhaps she was saying the same thing in another way with her last words, "There is only one
thing important in the world—that is love."

■

196-197 DeNully Hill, St. John, United States
Virgin Islands

afterword

The project of which this book is the result began early in 1975, when, at Hugh Stix's invitation, I took the subway downtown to 13 Vandam Street in New York's Greenwich Village. The house was just as Marguerite had left it, still alive with her presence, and nowhere was that presence so pervasive as in the studio. Though I had known her and much of her work for some years, I had had no idea of its variety and inner consistency.

As the atmosphere made itself increasingly felt, Hugh asked me if I would write about her and her art. I was already deeply involved with other projects, but such was the impression of the experience that I could not but agree. I began with a description of the studio as I saw it that winter morning, because it seemed to me then and still seems to suggest much about the private world of her creative imagination.

I am grateful to Hugh Stix for giving me the opportunity to embark on the project; to the many friends of Marguerite who have shared their remembrance of her with me; to the many photographers whose camera eyes have made it possible to reproduce episodes from her life and an overall view of her art from its beginnings; to Walter Vollmer, who translated letters and documents from the German; to Theresa Brakeley, whose sympathetic editing was but a part of her generous contribution; and to all the others who have worked with me on the project.

In particular I am grateful to Marguerite herself for all the works in many media with which it has been my good fortune to live in close association during the course of the writing. So that they may "speak for themselves in their own language" (as she put it in relation to the shells she loved), there are more

illustrations than pages of text, since it is the objects she created which are of
primary importance, rather than my words about them.
July 15, 1977

Richard McLanathan

198 Marguerite at work

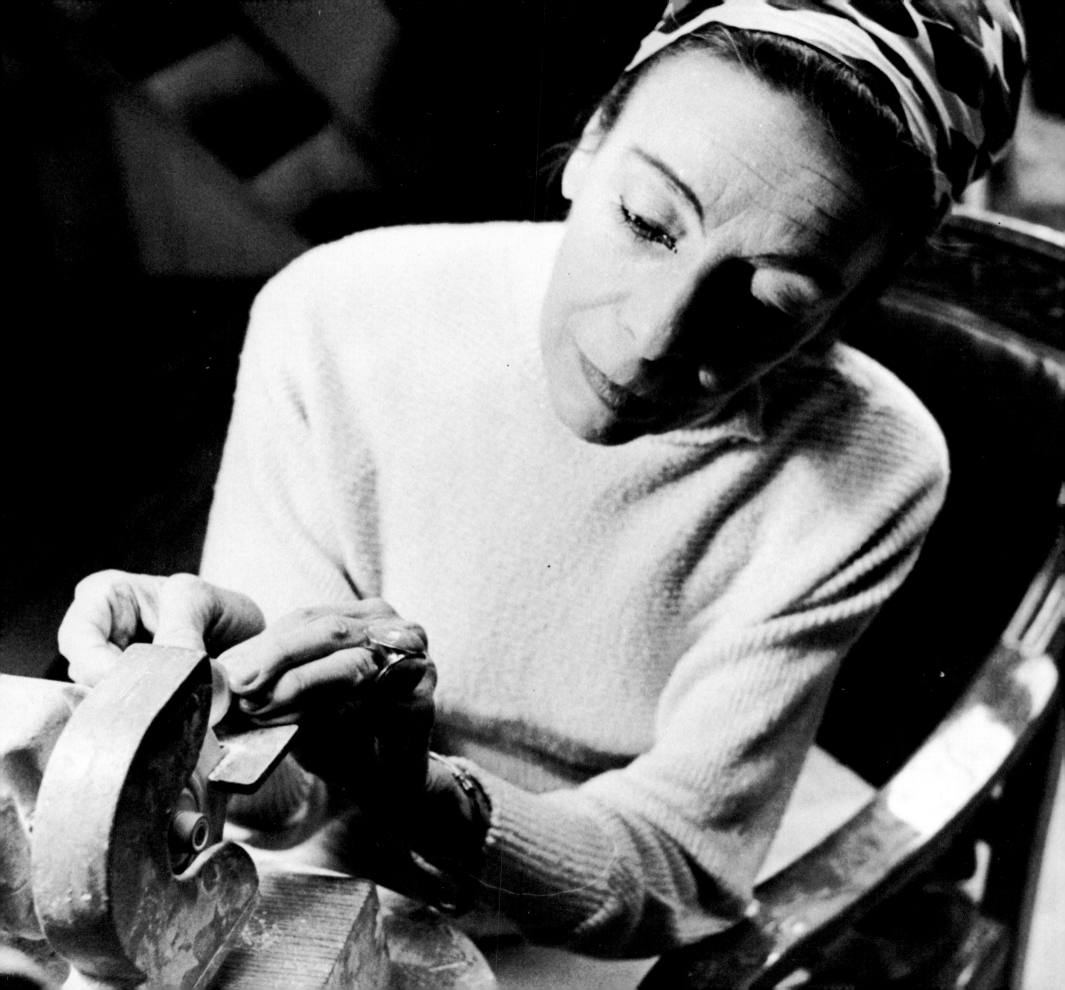

BIOGRAPHICAL OUTLINE

1907	Born Margret Christine Salzer, Vienna, Austria, June 15
1914	Sent to live with grandparents at Innsbruck, during World War I
c. 1923	Entered group surrounding Josef Hoffmann in Vienna. Went on to complete courses in arts and crafts at Kunstgewerbeschule
1925	Won prize for over-life-size ceramic figure at Paris World Exposition as pupil of Powolny
1925–1928	During visits to Paris studied at the Académie de la Grande Chaumière and in the studios of Despiau and Bourdelle
1928	Exhibition of Paris watercolors at Wiener Werkbundt and other galleries
1928–1938	Worked in Vienna as sculptor, ceramist, and designer of architectural and landscape decoration and exhibited frequently in major European cities
1938	Fled to Paris from Nazi takeover of Vienna, March 11. Designed ceramic pins, buttons, and other accessories for the *haute couture*
1940	Escaped from Paris one day ahead of Nazi invasion, June 10. Imprisoned in concentration camp at Gurs. Made drawings of the life of internees. Released July 19
1941	Arrived in the United States from Lisbon, April. Settled in New York City. Published account of her experiences, October
1941–1946	Worked in ceramics factories and in spare time created ceramic accessories, tiles, and boxes in her studio on MacDougal Street

1946	Gave up factory work and turned to painting and drawing, though continuing some ceramics
1949–1963	Concentrated on sculpture and assisted Hugh Stix with The Artists' Gallery
1951	First American exhibition of sculpture, under the name of Marguerite, at Bertha Schaefer Gallery
1956	The Stixes took the house at 13 Vandam Street, New York
1963	Turned from sculpture to the study of shells and design of shell jewelry
1964	First exhibition of shells, Vandam Street, March 1. Invention of stand for shell display
1964–1974	Many exhibitions of shell jewelry
1968	Publication of *The Shell: Five Hundred Million Years of Inspired Design*
1975	Died in New York City, January 10

LIST OF EXHIBITIONS

| 1972 | Cartier, New York City, May–June |
| | The Horse, Greenville, Delaware, October |

| 1973 | Cartier, Palm Beach, Florida, February |

| 1974 | Swan Ball, Nashville, Tennessee, June |

GROUP EXHIBITIONS

| 1925 | Exposition Internationale des arts décoratifs et industriales modernes, Paris: "L'autriche à Paris." Prize for over-life-size ceramic figure. |

| 1928 | W.iener Werkbundt, Vienna, and other galleries. Watercolors done in Paris |

| 1951 | Metropolitan Museum of Art, New York City, "American Sculpture, 1951," December 7, 1951—February 24, 1952 |

| 1952 | Whitney Museum of American Art, New York City, Annual.Exhibition: Sculpture, Watercolors, Drawings, March 14—May 4 |

| 1954 | The Pennsylvania Academy of the Fine Arts, Philadelphia, 149th Annual Exhibition of Painting and Sculpture, January 24—February 28 |

Whitney Museum of American Art, New York City, Annual Exhibition: Sculpture, Watercolors, Drawings, March 17–April 18

Knickerbocker Artists' Annual Exhibition, New York City

1956   Contemporary Arts Museum, Houston, Texas,
        "Monumentality in Modern Sculpture," December 13, 1956—January 13, 1957

1957   The Spiral Group Exhibition, The Artists' Gallery, New York City

1958   The Spiral Group Exhibition, Riverside Museum, New York City

1959   "Art: U.S.A.: 59": Coliseum, New York City, April 3–19

        Silvermine Guild of Artists, Silvermine, Connecticut,
        Tenth Anniversary New England Exhibition

        Spiral Group Exhibition, Hudson River Museum, Dobbs Ferry, New York

1960   Artists' Equity Showcase, New York City, April

        The Spiral Group Exhibition, New York University, New York
        City and Sunken Meadow, Long Island, New York

1963   Ball State Teachers College Art Gallery, Muncie, Indiana,
        Ninth Annual Drawing and Small Sculpture Show, March 7–31

NOTES AND BIBLIOGRAPHY

1. Diamonstein, Barbaralee, *Open Secrets: Ninety-four Women in Touch with Our Time.* New York: Viking Press, 1972, pp. 379–84. Summary of background and career; answers to questionnaire on attitude toward position of women and recent social problems.

2. Gomperz, Margret [Marguerite Stix], "Career in France," *Mademoiselle.* October, 1941, p. 90 ff. Narrative of concentration-camp experience, with illustration.

3. *The Headley Treasure of Bibelots and Boxes.* foreword and notes by George W. Headley, introd. by Guido Grigorietti. Milan: A. Manca Editore, n.d. [1973]. Catalogue in four languages with colorplate of a Marguerite Stix shell box.

4. *The New International Illustrated Encyclopedia of Art.* New York and London: Greystone Press, 1970, p. 4134. Brief outline of biography and career.

5. "Sea Gems," *Look.* July 27, 1971, p. 40. Brief text on shells and shell jewelry, with color illustrations.

6. *The Shell Desk Diary for 1974* and *for 1975.* n.p.: The Shell Oil Company, n.d. Ephemeral publications, but bearing biographical and career notes on Marguerite Stix and with good color reproductions of her jewelry.

7. Stix, Hugh and Marguerite, and R. Tucker Abbott, *The Shell: Five Hundred Million Years of Inspired Design.* New York: Harry N. Abrams, Inc., 1968 (paperback, 1972). The record of the study and creative activity that occupied Marguerite Stix and her husband from 1963 on.

INDEX

PHOTOGRAPHIC CREDITS

To the following photographers, who recorded over many years the exhibitions and celebrations of the art of Marguerite Stix, grateful acknowledgment is made by the publisher and the author: Ellen Auerbach, Oliver Baker, Joel Baldwin, Stephen Barre, Harry Bowden, Geoffrey Clements, Maxwell Coplan, Juke Goodman, Hiro, Otto Nelson, George Roos, Ben Ross. In addition, publication of pl. 158 is credited to the courtesy of The New York *Post* and that of pl. 198 to *Women's Wear Daily*.